Readers' voices

"All too often you see yet another 'how to' book and you just can't be convinced to spend your time absorbing that information. This book, however, combines hardliners and daydreamers, stimulating new ideas about the missing link: beautiful evocations to convert your brain."
STEPHAN J. WIRTZ, PROFESSOR FOR BUSINESS AT CORVINUS UNIVERSITY OF BUDAPEST

"*Beautiful Brains* is filled with wonderful wisdom for everyone interested in becoming a better human being and making a significant impact on society. The advice of her contributors is on point, and I love how Thy-Diep solidifies their lessons in for the reader with her brain brush exercises. I do not doubt that her contribution will help us change how we work together so we can change how we live together."
MICHAEL O'BRIEN, EXECUTIVE COACH, SPEAKER AND AUTHOR OF *MY LAST BAD DAY SHIFT: HOW TO PREVENT BAD MOMENTS FROM TURNING INTO BAD DAYS*

"Reading *Beautiful brains change tomorrow...today*, I welcomed each interview like a unique flower making up a beautiful and diverse bouquet of stories, experiences, and concrete recommendations for self-development.
Thank you, Thy-Diep, for the co-creation of this inspiring dive into the topic of leadership at an individual, business, and societal level! May it touch the hearts and minds of many leaders and leaders-to-be around the world!"
KATRIN GRUNWALD, ORGANIZATIONAL DEVELOPMENT CONSULTANT AND FOUNDER OF THE GLOBE TEAM

"With *Beautiful Brains*, Thy-Diep took me on a 'heartfulness' journey, filled with opportunities to candidly learn from execs, founders, artists, and other change-makers of our society, as to what mindfulness means to them. It has not only taught me the meaning of mindfulness but also helped me define my own inner peace."
CHUL KWON, GROWTH PRODUCT MANAGEMENT AT TURING

"A truly wonderful book, that inspires you to learn from the lives of others."
NIKOLAS KANONIS, SENIOR OPERATIONS MANAGER AT BURGER KING

"This book connected me to ideas, stories, and worldviews that left me happy and inspired. Human beings looking for uplifting models of a more fulfilling life will find much nourishment here."
MARC MACALUSO, SCREENWRITER

W0368545

co-created by Thy-Diep (Yip) Ta & Friends

BEAUTIFUL
BRAINS
CHANGE TOMORROW
... TODAY

Honest conversations with
change-makers leading heartful
ventures to transform business and society

Beautiful brains change tomorrow...today
Copyright © 2019 Thy-Diep Ta
All rights reserved.

ISBN: 978-3-9820846-2-6

Published by Thy-Diep Ta 2019

www.beautifulbrains.club
contact@beautifulbrains.club

No parts of this publication may be reproduced, stored in a retrieval system, or transmitted in any form or by any means, electronic, mechanical, photocopying, recording, or otherwise, without the prior written permission of the copyright owner.

This book is sold subject to the condition that it shall not, by way of trade or otherwise, be lent, resold, hired out, or otherwise circulated without the publisher's prior consent in any form of binding or cover other than that in which it is published and without a similar condition including this condition being imposed on the subsequent purchaser. Under no circumstances may any part of this book be photocopied for resale.

Cover design by Clara Seger
Interior design by Amie McCracken

To those who seek to find inner peace and shine their beauty to the world.

Proceeds from this book support projects that advance well-being for business and society.

Table of Contents

Yip's welcome letter

Dear beloved reader,

This book was written in an attempt to provide a colorful collection of beautiful stories. As I wrote my morning pages of December 20, 2018, I was wondering what it was that I had always aspired to do before turning thirty years old in February. It came to me that I had spent so much time searching for inspirational ways to live a good life. One where it is fun to wake up in the morning because you know that life will surprise you with many beautiful gifts throughout the day. Where you feel like your actions make sense because they contribute to something bigger than just your own life, something that you care about deeply. To me, this was about bringing joy to others, making workplaces healthier and happier places to be. Places where we do not waste our precious time, and then try to catch up on "life" during weekends and holidays but where work is invigorating and benefits our lives. I reached out to many wonderful leaders whose presence, their way of making decisions in their organizations, and the positive perspective they had on life and well-being had somehow left a strong impression on me. I asked them to co-create this book — a mindfulness manifesto, a space that contains personal stories of leaders who are courageous enough to share topics and ideas that feed into an unconventional approach entrepreneurship, leadership, and societal engagement. They are leaders who care about others' well-being, about the well-being of society and/or nature, and who have understood that in order to bring their best selves to the world, they need to also take good care of their own well-being. They have understood that we live in a deeply interdependent world, where we are all part of a system, that can only be transformed if we start transforming ourselves first.

The book has three parts: We have a section on personal transformation, one on transformation of our communities that we interact in, and the third part has views on how we can shape entire societies. The language chosen is a simple one, as we attempt to create a book that is serving not only our intellect, but also the soul. We shall feel nourished, reading the heartful sharings of the generous contributors. The #hashtags in the table of contents can give you additional information as to what this chapter will focus on. Each chapter ends with a short "brain-brush" exercise where we invite you to reflect about how these stories can be (or not be) part of your journey. It's the practice of seeing similarities and interconnection between two human beings. May you enjoy some moments of peace and warmth when you dive into these conversations.

Thank you to Peter-Paul de Leeuw from AmberScript for the use of your automated transcription services. I wanted to also say thank you to Amie McCracken, Tam Thi Tran, Constantin Maier, Clara Seger, Christian Zweckerl, Alla Golovanova, Martina Baur, and Bettina Engel-Gulba: without your generous help, this work would not have come to life.

In gratitude for sharing your time with us,
Yip
Thy-Diep Ta

About how Yip met the co-creators:

Cem Dinc, doctoral student in medicine and former player of the Turkish national basketball team:

Cem was introduced to me by my mentor, Thanh Long, with the words: This person will change the world… you need to listen to his story. And having afternoon conversations with Cem about life over a cup of tea has now become one of my most appreciated pastimes. Sometimes, we take our conversations outside, and I'm curious what others see when we walk side by side: him, 2.11m next to me, 1.55m.

Dat Phan-Angevin, founder at Cèdres Bleus:

To me, Anh Dat is a highly respected, spiritual elder brother. His capacity to listen is as vast as an ocean, his compassion and kindness in interaction with others and generous sharing of his learnings from the studies of Buddhist psychology and personal transformation are what I feel the corporate world can benefit very much from. He is an author, poet, artist, and teacher of Buddhist meditation.

Edward Sizzerhand Obika, founder of sizzerbees and DJ/Producer at Square One:

Eddie is a person of many talents. He pays strong attention to detail and yet is always focused on crafting the next big masterpiece which will blow your eyes, ears, and soul. I was an editor of his European online music platform, Hiphopjudge.com, where we put an emphasis on giving underground artists a voice.

Enrico Amiotti, executive vice-chairman, Enrica Amiotti Foundation:

Enrico has been my guardian angel for the past year, helping me connect with beautiful souls left and right on my path. I value very much his heartful and patient commitment to bring to life his mission of transforming the current education system into a joyful and healing experience of community and intuitive learning.

Dr. Hans Werner Hagemann, founder of Munich Leadership Group:

Hans is one of these senior consultants who have not only the intellect, but also the integrity and big heart to transform companies into organizations that care about ethics and the well-being of their individual members.

Jan Dzulko, founder of Everphone:

Speaking to Jan is always an exciting and rewarding experience. He loves to crack exotic problems, and he doesn't care about not conforming to the mainstream. He shows so much loving kindness to his family and friends. Having him as a friend is a blessing.

Julia Merkt and Michael Lubomirski, founders of Soulmastery and Soulartist:

Julia and Michael are a dream team, and I have rarely seen two people approaching meditation in such an entrepreneurial and authentic way. I love spending time exploring the meaning of life with them. Each time we meet, they share some of the newest meditation techniques they have found on their quest to understanding consciousness.

Karishma Adatia, PhD student in polymer chemistry and managing director of Akram:

Karishma is one of these very beautiful, bright shining lights that you meet once and will remember for a long time. She has a sharp mind, has been a business leader for most of her life, and yet, she speaks in a voice that resembles the flow of water. We met as undergraduate students as fellow scholarship holders from the Friedrich Ebert Foundation.

Karsten Nohl, founder and chief scientist of Security Research Labs:

Karsten and I met on a bus ride in rural Thailand. We were both on the way to a meditation retreat center, and during the ride we learned that we had both been part of McKinsey. Despite his great professional success, he has stayed down to earth and lives a humble life. He keeps a steady practice of enjoying the uncertainties of life and welcomes even uncomfortable situations with a warm smile.

Dr. Kerstin Humberg, founder of Yunel:

Kerstin was one of those people I knew I had to meet, having been told by three unrelated people (a partner from McKinsey, a partner from Aberkyn, and Muhammad Yunus) that she would be the one to connect to if I ever wanted to do any meaningful work in the area of self-development. They were right, and I hope we get to spend some more time together in the future.

Luca Urbano, founder at Food from Forest:

Luca is one of the wittiest and most genuine entrepreneurs I've ever met. He cares deeply about creating impact and setting up structures that are self-sustainable. What I appreciate very much about working with him is the love and enthusiasm he puts into his projects, and the rigour with which he pursues the endeavors.

Luis Hanemann, partner at e.ventures:

Luis was the Chief Marketing Officer at Rocket Internet in 2013, when I joined to develop the markets in South East Asia for one of the ventures. I was highly impressed by how open-minded he was towards his employees, and how he focused on serving in a way that was most helpful rather than telling others what to do.

Dr. Martin R. Stuchtey, founder and managing partner of SYSTEMIQ:

Martin was a senior partner on one of the first projects I had in McKinsey in 2014. I was a very junior team member, and still, Martin was always friendly and open. Martin loves to solve problems, in particular problems of grand societal impact, and he doesn't care who will be the other person solving the problem with him, as long as it is done, which I found to be a very pleasant attitude for collaboration.

Mika Schwarz, artist and lecturer at Academy of Fine Arts Leipzig:

Mika is a beloved friend whom I met at a transformative 21day retreat in Buddhist Plum Village monastery in Southern France. She is the one who made me understand that even in the crafting of arts, there is a structured process — it is not random, but a process of prototyping, and letting go, which reminded me very much of what it takes to be successful in business.

Nikolas Schriefer, founder at Stagelink:

I met Nikolas a few years back, at a national event for the start-up network (SUN) in Berlin. He is one of those entrepreneurs who dream big, but not for the sake of being rich and famous, but because they believe that their service offering will make the world a better place. And what is on top, he is not only a great entrepreneur, but also a trained musician, who is able to demystify the black box of music.

Philipp Heiler, founder at brainboost:

Philipp is not only a passionate medical doctor, but he also loves technology, neural networks, the brain, and becoming a great (social) entrepreneur. While Philipp is one of the fastest thinkers I have met, he cares equally about developing his and his team's social skills. I was so touched by seeing the way brainboost made children and parents smile that I asked him to let me join the company as a part-time member to help grow the brainboost community.

Dr. Ralf Schneider, group CIO of Allianz SE:

Ralf has been one of these very visionary thought leaders and most supportive clients and now friend that I have met along the way. He has a very sharp mind, and is a very humble and hands-on intra- and entrepreneur. What I really enjoy about our conversations is that he somehow manages to push my intellectual boundaries in a very respectful and encouraging way. It's always difficult to have Ralf join weekend events because he puts family first.

Sylvie Barbier, founder at Art / Earth / Tech:

Sylvie is not only an artist, she is also a very visionary entrepreneur who was the one who introduced me to the concept of co-creation. She radiates this loving, caring, and very generous energy, while being a highly structured and effective leader. She makes sure that every team member feels welcome and at home.

Dr. Tu-Lam Pham, founder of DigitalIQ:
Tu-Lam is my very smart and outspoken Vietnamese brother (from different parents), whom I look up to when it comes to seeing how to be funny, humble, and kind at the same time. He really cares about being a role model to the younger generation and finding ways to show society how to make good use of the opportunities of digitization.

Urs Merkel, founder at MatchManao:
Urs and I share this vision of making coaching a human right. We met at the Bits & Pretzels Startup conference in Munich, and it was something like a spark at first sight. It turns out that we both love hip Hop very much. Urs is one of the most helpful and inclusive human beings I have met.

Veronika Schweighart, founder at ClimedoHealth:
Veronika and I were classmates during our undergraduate studies in Global Business Management at the University of Augsburg. She is one of the few women I know who were courageous enough to follow the entrepreneurial path and found their own company after school. Veronika always has a smile when she meets you, and she truly embodies empathy and compassion in her leadership style.

Xiaowei Rose Luo, associate professor of Entrepreneurship and Family Enterprise at INSEAD:
Professor Luo was one of these rare professors at business school who made me reconsider my perspective on business leadership and decision-making. In her course, I learned what empathy and ethical thinking really imply for a business decision-maker. She always has an open ear to listen to the concerns and questions of her students, and she teaches with so much love.

Foreword
An introduction to beautiful brains

Enrico Amiotti,

executive vice-chairman, Enrica Amiotti Foundation

I met Yip's beautiful brain — and the rest of her beautiful and energetic personality — at the INSEAD Campus last October, when INSEAD decided to change for good, announcing to the world it wanted to become the first top global business school to take care of both business and society, since most business issues are societal ones, in an increasingly globalized economy. Yip had opened a WhatsApp messenger chat on emotional intelligence, which gathered a handful of INSEAD Alumni during the INSEAD Force for Good celebrations, including me. Our group meeting started with a meditation on the Fontainebleau campus, then thoughts went on in a digital way and in two face-to-face meetings with her in Milan and Davos. To tackle the task of writing the foreword to Yip's book, I have just finished an impromptu meditation on a TGV going all the way from Montpellier to Brussels.

Let's start with BEAUTIFUL.

The Amiotti Foundation ran an "Education for Beauty" competition in 2017 to select three school projects that would tie music or arts together with math or science. In ancient Greece, the ideal of καλός κἀγαθός (*kalòs kagathòs*), linked the beautiful and the good, while the great classical and renaissance geniuses — from Pythagoras to Leonardo and Michelangelo — were great artists, craftsmen, and scientists, all in one person. Einstein played a violin and walked in nature to get inspiration.

There is something profound linking ethics and aesthetics. A square like Piazza Navona; an anthropic landscape like Umbria's hills are beautiful and make you feel good. Beauty is related to calmness, balance, symmetry (all mathematical properties) but also to some originality, some striking and unexpected feature which looks (or sounds) unique but connects you in a way to some universal feeling. Like an iPhone or a Mac (the first time we saw them), or the $e=mc^2$ formula, a Nautilus shell unfolding a Fibonacci series, a Chopin Nocturne, or a new business concept like microcredit in India. And when you see an ugly slum (which slum isn't ugly?), a grey Soviet-style block of flats, or an industrial wasteland, you know immediately that it's not good for the people living there, and you can bet that the people who planned them — or have the power to change them but don't — are or were not good either.

So, what is a beautiful BRAIN?

Who is typically the owner of a beautiful mind? Yip interviewed many beautiful minds whose common denominator is their engagement to make the world a better place *around them*. After all, we cannot all make headlines but we all can — and should! — "*cultiver notre jardin*," following Voltaire's advice. Which may mean many significant and all-important things: cultivate our talents (our ground), clean the mess in and around us, trim the weak or dead branches, don't waste water and efforts, run a circular and sustainable ecosystem, and plant some beautiful seeds which will blossom one day when we are no longer around. This is particularly true with education, when planting the seeds, or, rather, preparing a fertile ground for the kid's talents to blossom, is the main business of the educational system. You may read the interviews of this book as the unfolding of conscious efforts of self-improvement and environmental improvement in different domains or jardins: from IT security to venture capital, from education to circular economy.

However, brain shouldn't be a limiting definition. Brain-intensive efforts should come with emotion-filled actions. IQ is easier to measure in tests, but EQ — the emotional intelligence factor — is more important to induce change and impact reality. The good news is that EQ can improve over time if you train yourself, while IQ is fixed as an adult. Most of the people interviewed by Yip would agree — and have felt in their lives — that going alone may let you go faster, but going with others will let you go farther. Emotionally connecting and involving people is paramount for any conscious and successful change or venture, as well as for maintaining our social assets as entrepreneurs or managers and — most importantly — as parents and companions. And we are back with beauty and goodness: it's beautiful to feel good and to make others feel good. There is no learning without emotion: we can only retain — for the good or the worse — what affected us. In a fast-changing world when plain information is readily available through the internet, it is important to learn (and unlearn!), rather than to stack content without emotional and/or practical relevance, which will become obsolete.

To be happy and successful, we adults should cherish the child inside us. Toddlers and very young children are filled with enthusiasm which comes from an unfiltered mind and heart, connecting immediately with people and situations, being always present in the moment, ready to learn by empathizing and going through trial-and-error. Enthusiasm comes from the Greek *én-theos* i.e., having a God inside: there is a divine, unstoppable sparkle in enthusiasm which comes from the heart not just from the mind. That's why I personally favor "heartfulness" over "mindfulness", and meditation on the heart, our own heart (see www.heartfulness.org).

CHANGE: What sort of change are we talking about?

πάντα ῥεῖ (*panta rei*), everything changes, or rather everything flows, said Eraclitus 2500 years ago. We change whether we like it or not, as any living thing, which includes families, companies, cities, nations. As you read this page, some 50 million cells per minute are dying and being replaced in your body, hundreds of people are dying and being born on our planet. The notion of change is related to some stability factor. You can't possibly change everything at one time. There are some rules and structures at work. And even when one may overturn a rule, the new rule is defined against the old one and must come to terms with the old status quo.

Changing personal status quo — you can call it expanding your own comfort zone — is not much easier than changing societal status quo: the only thing, as Yip's interviewees would agree, is this is your responsibility. All in all, the ironclad law of entropy rules: systems left unmanaged decay, and it takes more energy and effort to tidy up and structure than to pollute and destroy, or simply overlook. It takes a lot of inner and social leadership to create, co-create, and structure. But then, you are in tune with your soul when you follow your personal life purpose. And you'd better have one. The *fil rouge* linking all the people contributing to this book is: all have a personal life purpose, bigger than themselves, for which they are ready — and happy — to spend their time, their free time too.

My life purpose is to change the educational system in Italy and all the world, by connecting education with the inner self, and the inner self with personal and social happiness, through self-awareness, self-esteem, and self-compassion. All this starting from a very early age, from pre-school to young adulthood, making teachers and parents aware of the great responsibility — and opportunities — they have in shaping forever the mind and the heart of each new girl and boy. Neurosciences and epigenetics teach us that from zero (in fact, already in our mother's womb) to six to eight years of age, when the conscious mind isn't (well) developed yet, we get from the people around us most of the programming — and encouragement, and wounds — we will live with until death. Words are rooted in culture and the word root for education is *ex-ducere*, i.e., to bring forward what is already inside, to literally give birth as in maieutics, Socrates' educational style which was named after the midwife's acts. It is all inside us... let's bring it forward!

A newly born child has the ability to recognize and speak all the sounds of all languages of the planet, and to adapt to all possible environments. Growth comes with pruning and selecting those mindsets that are most relevant for our own environment but also come with declining creativity, often accelerated by educational systems that favor verbal versus non-verbal skills, structured and pre-digested notions versus discovery, academic versus hands-on education, individual versus group experience, abstract and visual and digital versus natural and personal and deep feeling experience. Good educational methods can inspire good managerial methods: the maieutic approach gives responsibility — and voice — to any worker at any level, allowing innovation to originate where the action starts. A warm and emotionally-smart environment is needed in companies well as in schools.

TOMORROW... TODAY:

A sense of urgency is needed as is an ethical call. In a fast-changing world of increasing complexity and connectedness, being late is being wrong, by being unfair to those whose lives could be changed for the better. "*Cultiver notre jardin*" means to stick with seasons and avoid delaying planting seeds. As in education, a new cohort of kids is passing through each grade yearly, so it is in corporate units around the world. Being lazy or unprepared teachers, mentors, or leaders creates damage. It's a pity. And pities are sins, unethical, and worth some form of punishment. As Martin Stuchtey says in his interview to Yip, "First, we have to make sure that we don't waste a single minute of our lives on things that don't matter to us or that don't contribute to the change we want to see. So find yourself an assignment, a job, or build your own company where you can live in harmony with this bigger picture. Let's not spend time from Monday to Friday on anything that does not pay toward something meaningful." Our life purpose, that is.

NOW, OUR COLLECTIVE CALL:

We feel better when we find a good sense — a broader, higher sense — in what we do. We are especially happy when we find something new which makes sense to us. A new endeavor, a new beautiful collective achievement. Something which clicks nicely in our brain and heart. It closes a loop. It all started in Fontainebleau and developed in Davos, at the INSEAD Force for Good campaign launch.

Here is my call: Let's change education — from kindergarten to business post-graduate education — and society with it, having good health, self-expression, responsibility and happiness as our compass. Let's support those, that already invest a large amount of their times into cultivating a sense of compassionate collaboration. Let's start to read — and finish reading — this book by connecting to our breath and our hearts for a few minutes. And then by shouting: Yip Yip Hurrah!

Introduction
Mindfulness as a roadmap for a well-rounded life

Dat Phan-Angevin,
founder at Cèdres Bleus

At Blue Cedars, the mindfulness center where I live with my family and residents in France, is the Semene River that runs along the 17th century Cistercian abbey — now our home and a place for people to come and be embraced and nurtured by the beauty of nature, the warmth of community, and the quiet depths of solitude. In the river, there are smooth and well-rounded pebbles shaped, centuries after centuries, time after time, by the constant flow of water. Each of them perfect in their place, harmonious with the world. Life is constantly calling us back to the present moment to rediscover this harmony that perhaps we have abandoned in our childhood. Change-makers and leaders around the world are invited to listen deeply to their deepest aspirations in order to birth a new paradigm for the benefit of all living beings. Despite this harmony around us, for too long in our human history we have been threatened by fear and discrimination, focusing mainly on our differences — race, nation, gender, age, and so on. In the shadows of our modern progress and democracy, we have unconsciously conditioned an individualistic culture with people who live too much in their heads instead of their hearts. Our modern society is based on compartmentalization. We have been educated to specialize in one subject and neglect the rest. In this separation, we have divided ourselves from nature, from others, and sadly from our deeper self. There is no harmony. There is a broadcast called NST (non-stop thinking) that prevents us from connecting intimately with the mountains and rivers, the colors of a flower, or the beauty of a face. For too long, we have sharpened the intellect and worshiped thinking — echoing Descartes, "*Je pense donc je suis.*" (I think therefore I am.) One of the shadow elements of this mental habit is the division between "us" and "them." The result is ecological, social, and existential crisis — hence the urgency of an integral approach to remind us to see reality as an undivided whole and not only as individual parts, to integrate every aspect of being to reach a higher state of living. How can we be just like that well-rounded pebble — in peace and stillness where we are, to take our joyful place in the world?

Mindfulness is to be aware of both the inner and outer world. The Chinese character of mindfulness (nian, 念) has two characters. The top one signifies, *the present moment*, the bottom one, *the heart*. The closest English translation is not *mindfulness* but perhaps *heartfulness*. Hence, the present moment is not only to be aware of where we are in time and space, but it eventually includes and embraces a world view that touches on our common humanity instead of focusing on our differences. This insight opens the door to compassion. Therefore, I suggest we use the word, *heartfulness* instead of *mindfulness*. To be mindful is to become aware of ourselves and our environment. First, I may be aware of my steps and my breath, then my emotions and my perceptions. Then the blue sky and the wind. I may see that I am walking in the contemplative garden at Cedres Bleus. As my awareness expands, I realize I am in France. As it continues to open, I see that I am walking on the Earth. And at some moment, the division between myself and the world is erased as these are just mental concepts. It is like taking a plane high up in the sky and seeing beyond borders and frontiers. I am the world; the world is me. Or as the philosopher Spinoza contemplates, "The earth is one organism."

There is an old parable in the Buddhist canon about a father and son. After some relational conflict at home, the son decides to leave out of anger and spite. The night before he leaves, the father, a wealthy landowner, out of love and compassion, opens a seam in his son's jacket and hides a jewel. In case of times of trouble, the father hoped that the son would be assured by its presence. The son eventually settles down in a village far away and has his own business. A period of success comes, but war, drought, and famine finally take it all away. His business collapses, and he wanders like a hungry ghost. After years of hardship and suffering, the son, out of quiet desperation, decides to drown himself in a river. Before doing so, he sobs and takes his coat to wipe his tears. There he feels the hidden jewel inside. He realizes his father's unconditional love and goes back home. On return, he is greeted by his father with open arms.

We may realize, like the destitute son, that we have quite an abundance already around us and inside of us — that we are already whole and perfect beings and there is absolutely nothing to add or subtract. As mindfulness (or heartfulness) practice is taking its place in the secular world in the domains of neuroscience and research, health, education, and business, we need a right view of how to apply the practice in different aspects of life — to be more well-rounded like the pebbles in the river. Sophisticated instruments and complex ideas can help mold our technological and material world, but we need to keep things simple. So simple our mind could entirely miss it. We need to look within. Inquiring within is not what our modernity has taught us. It has become an unconscious habit to look outside of ourselves for happiness and solutions to our malaise. If you wish to find gold or diamonds, however, you must dig deeply.

Mindfulness is the foundation for concentration, and concentration leads to insight. I designed a map to help us visualize the paths we need to tread to find a balance. But this map is not about achieving each of the four things, it is about finding the place in between that allows for them all to exist. These four different types of mindfulness rely on each other and also on the self at the very center of it all. The graph contains two dimensions: a vertical plane (go deep and go high), and a horizontal plane (expand into social structures).

It points at the necessity to first deepen our understanding and care for our *self* at the core. In order to understand ourselves, we need to understand our body, sensations, emotions, perceptions, and consciousness. To go very far, we need to start very close. We need to look within. We wish to shed the skin of our false self to finally embody our true self. Or as the Italian artist, Michelangelo eloquently expressed, "I saw the angel in the rock and I liberated her." In this book, Philipp Heiler's interview reminds us of the importance of attending to the self as a mental hygiene; to add to our physical hygiene; to take care of our brain in the way we brush our teeth — moving towards cultivation of positive qualities of mind — serenity, joy, empathy, etc. as a regular practice and trainable skill.

Integral Mindfulness:
A map for a 4-fold personal path

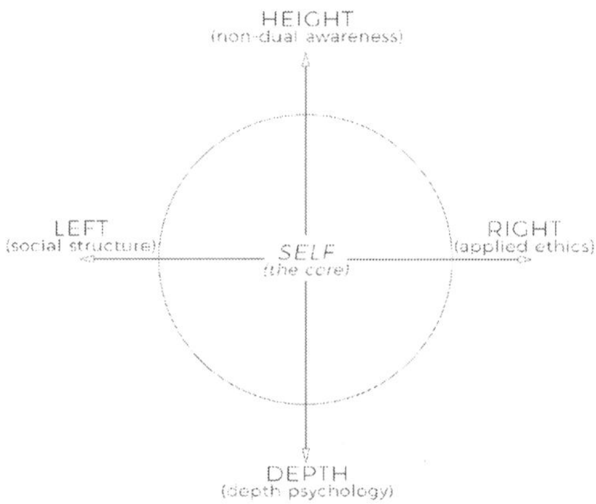

In addition, there are four dimensions of what I call the 4-fold integral mindfulness path, and they are mapped along two axes:

- **Depth – depth psychology:** inquiring within to heal cultural and personal wounds to prevent history from repeating itself.
- **Height – transcendence or non-dual awareness:** practices that help us go beyond our limited perception of the world and self.
- **Left-width – social structure:** practices to reorganize family, social structures, and our relationship to nature to align with our values and needs.

- **Right-width – applied ethics:** values that drive our intentions, thoughts, words, and actions toward the good, the true, and the beautiful.

The vertical axis displays dimensions of self-discovery and understanding who we are in a more universal context. Sylvie Barbier's interview in this book, for example, seeks reconciliation and healing, directly related to depth psychology, on exploring wounds and traumas. She shares how we could control our choices and follow through. We can also use some types of mindfulness practice to transcend ourselves. *The vertical axis is a key to being in good community with ourselves.*

The horizontal axis displays dimensions of social structures and applied ethics. There are practices that help us express ourselves in society, and doing so with a stable foundation grounded in ethics. Xiaowei Rose's vision for an inter-connected system shares about the importance of ethics and social well-being in an organizational setting, demonstrating the relevance of the horizontal axis for a well-rounded life. Throughout history, there have also been collective movements led by great figures, like Mahatma Gandhi, Nelson Mandela, Dr. Martin Luther King, and Thich Nhat Hanh, that have reminded us to continue to tread on the path of love and understanding. These men are honored, for they were able to join the collective in a common cause without any exclusion. As we now live in a global community, we need more and more conscious leaders that can look in this same direction to help usher in a new paradigm of functioning on all levels — individual and collective. As you will read in this book, you will see that the torch of our ancestors is still alive and burning in the hearts of these embodied leaders and change-makers around the world. *The horizontal axis is a key to being in good community with others, and with nature.*

Ultimately, none of the dimensions should be neglected in order to pursue a life of well-rounded mindfulness. When we are nourished by the energy of love, compassion, joy, and serenity, we liberate our highest potential as a human being. It takes much devotion, effort, and heartfulness. The key to reading this book, and finding the "correct" view, the right path, is the reflection process. You cannot simply take in wisdom and expect it to change your path. Every once in a while, you need to pause and take a step back to revisit this roadmap of life. This requires reflection — a skill that can be cultivated in the art of skillfully, mindfully, and heartfully reading. After each chapter, I invite you to take a moment and ponder. In which way do the stories relate to you? Where is your center in the moment, and is it balanced? In which dimension do you need work? How can you take steps forward to make change in your own life and others'?

Part One:

How to Become Your Own Best Friend

Sometimes just a little twist to your perspective can move mountains

Mika Schwarz,

artist and lecturer at Academy of Fine Arts Leipzig

What is currently most relevant to you?

I consider the relationship between self-doubts and producing arts to be very relevant; it's a theme that I encounter a lot in my private circle of friends — who are also artists, but also when talking to my students who are just starting to work artistically. When it comes to the arts, people tend to have very different opinions. Even experts have differing opinions depending on the context they operate in or the school they come from, and often one ends up completely confused about what to do when receiving so much differing feedback. With some years of experience, I am now really sure that the only way to progress in this profession is to find a way to rely on your own judgment. This means you need to find a way to remain calm and build confidence in your own judgment. It's easier said than done.

What is the purpose of arts for you?

My purpose as an artist is to change perspectives. I try to find a way to shift our views towards our environment. When you can change perspectives, you can change society. I come from a visual background; I'm a photographer by training. What I aim at is to convey this fresh, playful gaze of a child through my work. I try to inspire you to look at conventional things or commodities from a new perspective.

When I was a child, maybe around five years old, there was this night when I was in bed and felt very lonely. My mother was in the living room next door. The door was slightly open so that the light fell into the darkness in an upside down L-Shape. There was also a little triangle at the top of the door. To me it looked like a stork that was watching over me during the night. It helped me overcome my fears and my loneliness at night. It was just a little twist, and it wasn't really changing anything tangible, only the perspective, and yet it changed a lot. I think kids automatically try to find different views on things in order to make uncomfortable situations more bearable. For my current artwork, this principle is really important. Sometimes there are situations you can't really change easily, such as economic conditions. Don't get me wrong, I'm not saying that just changing the perspective is always sufficient. When we have a war going on, the war won't resolve just because we look at it in a different way. But while we are doing something against it, we still need to find ways to make life more bearable. I'm not too fond of using arts as a political vehicle. I think there is a fine line between arts in terms of introducing a point of view and propaganda in terms of using art to state a (subjective) truth. With arts, you can help people get a fresh gaze onto their life and mobilize the resources to drive a change. It's just a little nudge, a playful way for going back to your original nature, to finding your inner child.

How do you develop your own style?

I am always critical of the common phrase "my artwork talks about..." It limits artistic work, indicating that art functions as a metaphor, giving a clear thought a different shape, but I think that leads to missing out on the greater freedom of artistic work. So I'm trying to find a way to give an artistic suggestion for a specific topic, about something that relates to society, but that does not necessarily have to adhere to the real conditions and rules of society.

I currently work on transforming objects into pictures of objects. I have a garden table that has been outside in my backyard for quite some time. And when I looked at it one day, I saw something like a portrait on it. This caught my interest. It reminded me of when you are a child, and you look at clouds and suddenly see a dragon or a dinosaur in the sky. I wondered: What is the cognitive mechanism behind it? Has anybody ever written about it? I went online and researched "phenomenon seeing forms in clouds." I found out that in psychology this phenomenon is called *Pareidolia*. It is a greek word. *Para* means besides. And *Eidolon* means object. It's about looking beyond the real cloud to see a dragon. And then I wondered: What have psycho-analysts written about it? So I went to the library and dove deeper into the research. And this is when I began my artistic trials. I took off some layers of the garden table to uncover the portrait I had seen, just a little bit, to make it a bit easier for other people to see what I had seen. And then I thought, maybe I can apply this process to different objects and create something like my own artistic tool box. You see, the way I create my artwork is an intertwined process between research and trials. Thorough research adds depth to my artistic trials and it helps me build confidence because I know my work comes from a place of knowledge as well as sharpens my spoken and artistic language.

I love this moment when I'm in my studio and I have reached a point of understanding a specific topic of interest that I had been researching for a while. This is the moment when I feel that I have enough understanding to add my artistic contribution or lend my gaze to a topic that can maybe produce a shift in how others view this topic. I know my work is done when I feel that I've found a solution to communicate my work in a way where it can talk by itself without me being there and explaining it.

I see feedback as a suggestion of another person for me to improve my work. But I'd say there is this risk of sometimes consulting with others too early. And when this young work of yours is confronted with a lot of different questions about the content, about the goal, about your timeline and so on, it might just be completely overwhelming. Therefore it's very important that each person finds a balance of their own between exposure to questions and criticism and the state of unhindered development.

How do you discern nourishing feedback from destructive feedback?

For me, it's important to feel that the other person cares enough about my work so that they are really trying to dive into the details and understand it entirely. I consult only with a very limited number of people, maybe three or four, who I consider mindful listeners. These are people who are careful in their expressions, people who have undergone different stages of doubt themselves and who have produced great works with a lot of patience. In a way, they should care about my interest, not only about the artwork's interest. In addition, they need to be experienced enough in one area that is relevant to me in order to be able to put my work into the right perspective. When somebody has twenty years of experience in specific fields, and they have something to say about my work, I can't ignore their expertise. I can tell if somebody is an expert in what they are doing by the precision of their language. Useful feedback is very concrete. When people do not really care, they tend to use very vague language. Feedback that is not precise is all over the place, random. Sometimes they compare my work with other artists' works and then they just stop there. It's a little bit of a narrow perspective, and this shows me that they do not want to go the extra mile to understand my work. In the arts it's very important to also look at the evolution of an artist to understand how this piece of work has grown in its context.

Sometimes, after an exhibition, you get very different voices, and not all of them are positive voices. It's very important in these cases to discern between experts' critique and lay audience views. Some of my artist friends' work is very avant-garde, and for the lay audience, it's difficult to put it into context. If you attach too much to what you hear, it may destabilize your well-being.

When I had a first draft of my last work ready a while ago, I reached out to two mentors of mine for their feedback. One is a well known photography artist. She had a very photography-oriented view on my work. She suggested taking photographs of the object rather than displaying it, so as to make my process more clear to the viewer. The other person, artist Julian Göthe, had quite contrary feedback. He suggested focusing on the object itself and seeing in which way it filled the space. I sat at home and was quite confused. I had to step back and look at their feedback from a different perspective. I tried to understand their main interest in my work. Somebody who is a photography expert sees something different in my work than someone from the object field. When I looked at their feedback and put it in relation to my own work and my own interest, I could open up to their feedback. This process of inquiry also taught me something about my work; it showed in which way my work resonated with them. There were some aspects of their feedback that I had already thought about before hearing from them; and when they brought up the same things in their assessment, it's a signal to work on it. And then there is the element of care. I know that they really care, and this helps me to open up to their feedback and say, "Ok, from my point of view, their feedback is helpful for my next exhibition. I can take some photographs of my objects, and at the same time display the real objects in the same exhibition." Some people would call it a compromise, but I want to emphasize that it's much more than that. It's a productive way of taking different options into consideration and making good use of the available space, my background as a photographer, and my interest in objects. By opening up and integrating their feedback into my work, I was able to create a new artistic pathway, a narrow space in between photographic images and objects that was very different from what both of them do. In essence, as an artist, you really need to find your own position and rely on your judgment, otherwise you get lost in other people's views. When I receive multiple sets of feedback, I note it, step back, and try to place it into the context of the feedback provider. This helps not to take it too personally, not to take it to heart. It's just one view of one other person, and I see how it fits into my way of thinking or method of producing art before I integrate it. Ultimately, in arts, you should not try to make it "right" for another person.

How do you deal with failure?

This is also a question I get a lot from my students, who are at the very beginning of their artistic journeys. They mostly want to know how to develop ideas, and how to keep up the motivation for pursuing these ideas despite failures. When I start the research on a new arts project, I feel really excited about it and I try to find out as much as possible in a very short time period. There was a project in 2017 where I came across an archive of NASA that I found really fascinating. So I started to research a lot about it, and I got to a point where I had almost reviewed the entire archive and built up a lot of knowledge and enthusiasm about it. I then try to find some visual forms to transfer what I have experienced without being too plain about it. It's not cooked, you know? So after I have applied my artistic methods on this topic, and I look at the result, and they don't look great, I feel disappointed. As with the NASA case, I had to admit to myself that there was no way for me to enrich this archive. It just stood by itself. My methods or skills were just not sufficient at that point in time to make it become my own work. So I had to stop. I know that I should stop when I have the feeling that I have no ideas or tools to form a work out of what I see. Sometimes things are just interesting as they are, but I can't really add any of my artistic work to it. You're in your studio for weeks, every single day, trying to go somewhere and then you see that the result is null. It's super frustrating. What I then do is try to distance myself. Most of the times I have several projects in parallel, so I can turn to another project and direct my energies somewhere else for some time so as to escape from stagnation and frustration by keeping my workflow. You need to keep moving so you can break free from stagnation. I also talk to other artists, and most of the time, somebody else is also experiencing something similar. And I try to tell myself that it's quite natural, this process of being stuck. I work in the arts, and it's not a highway, it's an artistic path that I'm creating. I grew up in nature, in the mountains. And sometimes, the path just suddenly ends, and all you are left with is the woods. And the only thing you can then do is get back to the main path, if you're not ready to deal with the chaos. I still have all the NASA research in my folders, so at some later point in my life, maybe when I have other tools or a fresh mind, I can come back to try it one more time.

What do you want to share with the world?

Many people, in particular in my field, suffer from self-doubt. I don't know if it applies to every profession, but in my profession, the way out of suffering is finding a way to train or relate to your gut feeling. In my view, it's best to go back to my very basic start, take it easy, and not start with all the layers of complexity. Just start with something small, something basic, and then play around. Try to find what it is, that caught your interest about this idea in the first place. And do some research. And then you experiment a little bit. This is important. You have to start producing at some point in time, just little trials, otherwise you get stuck in research. And then listen to your gut feeling. You can be courageous in your exploration. There might be some interesting impulse that pops up during your research that may be more interesting to follow. That might lead to surprising works for yourself and for others.

And most important is to be as honest with yourself as you can possibly be, in order to understand why you do what. That makes it easier to understand your actual interest, even if that sometimes leads to admitting that your idea is less clever than you wished. But it brings you closer to yourself and makes you more stable towards the art market or trends.

Of course it is really rewarding when a curator tells you that they want to work with you because your work is great, but honestly, enthusiasm about your work and critique of it, they come and they go. Finding your personal passion and a way to transfer it into work, into your contribution to the world, can keep you going in the long run.

Beautiful brains change tomorrow...today
Brain-brush reflection exercise:

How did I feel when I read this?

What did I learn?

What will I integrate into my daily life?

How we can transform our fears

Sylvie Barbier,
founder at Art / Earth / Tech

What topic is currently on your heart?

My heart... I've recently embarked on a powerful personal transformation journey. I have come to realize that what I wake up for in the mornings is to find ways of transforming fear into unconditional love in myself and all around the world. To see people being united. Not only united in the sense that I bring people into my heart, but also physically united — united with family. I put families first because how we relate to our parents, brothers, and sisters is often the blueprint of how we relate to other human beings. When you can transform families, you can transform anything. It's a miracle, and as long as we're alive, miracles are possible.

I went to meet my brother for the first time in fifteen years of separation. His relationship with our dad was strained, and I remind him of our dad. I grew up feeling incomplete, because part of my family had disappeared from my life. It always felt like something was missing, and I felt powerless, not knowing what to do about it. I would tell myself: "One day, some day, my brother and father will heal their relationship and then I'll get to see him." But that one day became one year, two years… and before I knew it, it was fifteen years.

So about three years ago, I was experimenting with my self-development, and I attended this course called "Landmark Forum." There I literally saw how people would transform and begin talking to family members for the first time in a long time. This struck me. If they could do that, there was hope that I could do that too! To be fair, my breakthrough moment didn't just happen overnight. It was a challenging journey.

After the forum, I started to write letters to my brother. What made it difficult, was that I had this mindset, "It takes two to tango." We hear this everywhere, this 50/50 mindset: We expect that we only do 50% of the work, and that the other person will chip in the other 50%. This is not how life works! Besides, I find it to be imprisoning. It implies putting our freedom into the hands of others. With this mindset, if I wrote a letter, and my brother didn't answer, the natural reaction for me would be to stop my activities. But I had been longing to be reunited with my brother, and I didn't want to be stopped. So I was looking for something that would enable me to go all in. I needed to find a way that would allow me to still feel complete, even if my brother wouldn't answer. And I started by declaring that I'd go all in with this relationship. And I had to understand, if I wanted to have this extraordinary wish fulfilled, I'd need to stop being normal and step up to become extraordinary. So I wrote a letter to him that said: "Hey, I do want to know you. I want to be in your life. I want to get to know you. And so I'm coming."

When I rang the doorbell, my sister-in-law opened the door, and she was surprised. I saw three little girls running around joyfully; three beautiful souls that I had never met because I had always been so scared. I was overwhelmed by the emotions that came when I realized I had missed out on six years of their lives, and on fifteen years of my brother's life, because I had waited for the tango to start. What is even more powerful is this experience has also helped me heal the relationship with myself: I now know I am fearless. Just the mere fact that we stood face to face is something I consider a miracle. It was a tangible experience — not a whimsy of my mind. For the past few decades, it has been my biggest fear to see my brother. And now, having gone through it, it feels like whatever comes next in life will be easy.

You could have gone there and the door was shut or nobody was at home...

The fears are totally there, and they never go away. I had no idea if my brother was going to be there. I told him the date that I was coming because I wanted to give him the opportunity to not be there in case he chose so. I didn't mean to impose myself on him, but I wanted to say "I'm here to show you with my action, how much I care." The situation was very awkward. When you haven't seen a person for fifteen years, it's not like you'll jump for joy and embrace each other. When my brother came down and saw me, he was trembling with fear. He said, "Fifteen years ago I decided to cut all the Barbiers." And the words he used, they were so scary for me too, because they referred to me, his sister. I felt emotional. But since I had committed to come there to tell him that I loved him and to accept him whoever he was, I was unstoppable. I think it was important to mean it, that I hadn't come to fix him or to fix this situation. It didn't matter at all what he said, I was ready to listen. And I felt such a beautiful shift in my being, in my relationship towards myself.

Sometimes, I still have a little voice coming up, telling me nasty things about myself and about others. But my commitment to transforming my fear into unconditional self-acknowledgement and love is way bigger than the fear that comes from the need for protecting myself. So transformation of fears requires putting things into a context. When this context is something meaningful enough it touches your heart and other people's hearts, it can become bigger than yourself, and it can be powerful enough to silence the little voice of your ego.

I believe all of us know our context when we're born. You can actually see the context in every kid. When you speak to children, they tell you things like "I want to save the world," or "I want to be a musician." I see it as a gift that we are given and that we, as kids, want to contribute to the world. Our context is with us all the time. The sad thing is that along the path of growing up, we forget about our gift. So we have to go find it again, remove all the surrounding crap, and become who we are the way we already were, when we were born. We were born beautiful beings, perfect beings, with these gifts ready for touching the world! Some days, you may think, "Am I sure? Is this still the right path?" and that's totally fine. We need to be willing to go on a never-ending journey of self-discovery and self-development to relate to it or renew our relationship to this bigger picture.

What is your contribution to the world?

My husband Rufus, our friends Ninon, Liam, and I, together with some more people, have founded an organization called Art/Earth/Tech where we research something we call the "collective blind spot." For example, events like the elections in Brazil, Trump, Brexit, or the gilets jaunes in France are things that surprised some of us. They were there, but we didn't acknowledge them because they were in our collective blind spot.

So what we do is try to understand the root causes of our blind spots, literally to understand what makes us act the way we're acting. The society we live in is a little bit uninspired. Just think about the introduction of the first iPhone: iPhone 3 — wow! Then iPhone 4, 5, and so on, and now, we have gotten so used to it — it's cool, it works well, but nothing new anymore, right? Only incremental innovation. And the cycle we are in right now with our society, it's not so different. It's incremental — there is no new big vision. Politicians like Macron or Barack Obama were probably more competent than the previous presidents, and their management might have been more effective, but when you listen to them, it's all about reducing risk and being more efficient. The only ones who are offering some new big vision to cater to the real cravings of society are the radicals at the left or the right.

In general, I think there is definitely a blind spot around community and spirituality. In our view, the model of individualism has led to loneliness, depression, and even an increase in suicide rates. Hence, the need for community. Many of us still associate spirituality or religion with oppression, or with believing in "Father Christmas." The way we are being taught about religion is infantile. We are asked to believe that there is a God who created the world in seven days. This makes it difficult for people to talk openly about their faith; a person who openly says "I believe in Christ," more often than not puts herself at risk for being looked down upon. Additionally, in the western world, there is fear of committing to being part of a group or community, because we think they might brainwash us or that we will be isolated from society.

As long as we don't free ourselves from our blind spots, we're stuck — there is no safe space to discuss faith in public; and no space to discuss any kind of community in public. I can't stop stressing the importance of us needing to overcome our fears, because if we want to solve big global challenges like climate change, we need to get together and take collective actions! We can't solve them as individuals. We have to heal our collective trauma as a community, and we need to give space to spirituality in our lives because it takes some level of spirituality to understand what we are actually doing to mother Earth right now in order to solve climate challenge.

With our work, we hope to create a new vision for our century that embodies spirituality and community, and grounded in research. We also organize conferences, gatherings, and so on, where we bring people together to share their views and have an honest and intellectual conversation about wisdom. In addition, we engage in something I call the "lived conversation in community." We're experimenting with transforming real estate into conscious co-living hubs across Europe where you can try out and experience these intellectual concepts. We try to provide solutions that go beyond duct tape solutions. It's more than just creating a group that cleans up the beaches from time to time. We're aiming at finding sustainable models that are alternatives to our current individualism model.

So in our co-living hubs we aim at developing ways of living that are not optimizing for efficiency or practicality only but that nourish our souls. If I lived by myself, I could choose when and what I want to eat, go see my friends the days I want to see them, listen to music as loud as I wanted to, and so on. In our co-living community, for example, we decide to eat twice a week together. This means that on Wednesday evenings, I can't just go to meet my friends because I made a commitment to contribute to community life by sharing my presence with the community members.

It's a conscious trade I engage in: I give up some part of my individual freedom, and in return, I receive freedom from loneliness. When I feel lonely or sad, I know there is somebody to listen to me, and maybe even hold my hand. I'd say something like, "I'm not feeling well, and there is something in my way, something inside me causing me suffering and I'm not able to see it." If you feel unwell, speak out. Do not keep it in your head because the mind can be a dangerous place. And if you still choose to dive deep into your head to understand what's in there, don't go on this journey alone. Take someone with you, so they can pull you out. To me, having this mental support is more valuable than the freedom to leave my socks on the table whenever I want.

Spirituality is linked with the concept of inter-being — what we do is also impacting our surroundings. Living in a community is a good way to practice this view of the world. If we want to co-exist peacefully on this planet, we need to go beyond our individual egos. Community means to co-live in a way where we understand you are part of me, and I am part of you. This can be extremely challenging because it can push you out of your individual comfort zone.

How do you make sure that the rules that you set in the community don't turn into dogmatism?

This question is just fascinating in itself! The first thing you jump into is a hypothetical worry — the fear that being in a group will lead to dogmatism. It's something I have experienced to be a collective trauma of community, so deeply rooted in our consciousness, that the moment we mention groups, people start to get antsy. It's a big leap to jump from, "You can't leave your socks on the table" to "one day, you'll be sacrificing all your freedom and be brainwashed." I have this automatic fear response too, in particular, when I spend time in community models including the Buddhist Plum Village community, or any other events with large groups of people. Feeling fear is actually also a loss in freedom: we don't get to choose if we feel afraid, it typically just happens based on how we were brought up. It makes sense we have this reaction, if we reflect on the dangerous history with the Nazis, the Inquisition, and any other religious, political, or spiritual formations or oppressive organizations and asked their members to do harmful things.

So in order to let go of this collective trauma, you need to go out and seek conversations with people who you would be scared of talking to. Or with those whom you don't talk to because you fundamentally disagree with their views. You need to listen to them without any judgments. The moment people feel someone has listened to them, they open up and are also ready to listen. That's the starting point of a beautiful conversation. The most dangerous thing that happens is when you stop talking to each other. It's like a wall in between two people. I see that with my family. My father and brother don't speak. It's difficult to move anything when there is no communication because the person on one side of the wall is restricted in imagining what the other person thinks. Why do we make life so complicated?

As long as you keep the communication line open, things can evolve. Even if the line is bad, it's better than none because you still keep the possibility to grow something from it. Of course, it's much better if you speak with love, but even if it's just much shouting and screaming and crying, it's better than nothing. When I speak with people who are completely different, I often realize "Oh my God, there's a whole other world out there," which somehow nourishes my soul.

So if you can honestly answer: "Of course, I won't let this happen because I'm not the type of person who will be quiet when something harmful happens!" you don't need to fear loss of freedom in a group. It's important that you trust yourself first before you can go and live in a community because you need to trust yourself to trust a group. I can choose a different manifestation of myself through a different way of acting. A cat just gets to be a cat, but we are human beings who can consciously decide when we want to stand straight on our two feet, grounded on the Earth. Consciousness is when we take the responsibility to see who and where we currently are and to start looking into how we actually want to be. We live our freedom by choosing actions that are consistent with who we want to be. It is something uniquely to human beings in a way it requires an action to stand up. It's nothing passive, and, just as a muscle, we need to train it for it to be strong.

I know it sounds crazy, but I think it all boils down to having faith. Having faith doesn't need to have an object. It's an experience! I don't ask you: "Do you believe in sex?" When you experience an orgasm, you don't need to believe in it anymore. It's the same with love. You experience it. The moment you try to capture it, it goes away. It's a little bit like trying to catch chickens or bunnies. They just run away, the moment you run after them. Faith is that moment when you surrender to pure experience. At that moment, you experience something beautiful, and it's also when it becomes needless to say "I believe in beauty." Most of the times, when I'm suffering, it's because the actions I choose to take don't go hand in hand with who I choose to be. In the end, it comes down to seeing who we are currently choosing to be and having faith that we can become this person.

How do we become good members of the Earth community?

We are earthlings. Earth is our home, or, it's even more than that, it's like our mother. Therefore, we should treat it the same way we treat our mothers: with love and respect. Currently, we live in a beautiful organic flower farm close to Paris. It's called "La Chéraille." Christophe, the owner, he taught us how to grow our own fruits and vegetables, and it's just mesmerizing to see how abundant the Earth is.

For me, the way we treat the Earth is just a reflection of how we treat ourselves. When we pollute our rivers, the toxins will ultimately end up in our own bodies. Our actions mirror the love that we have for ourselves. I love this quote by a drag queen called RuPaul, who says, "If you don't love yourself, how the hell you gonna love somebody else?" And he's so right. If you don't love yourself, how can you love mother Earth?

Equally important for taking good care of our Earth, is to stop judging ourselves for our actions. Yes, if we look at all the pollution we are causing, and all the big cities we are building up that contribute to accelerating climate change, from mother Earth's view, we are probably not better than termites. However, the moment we judge ourselves for our behavior, we will not enjoy the blessings of mother Earth in this present moment. And it's also important to understand that one day, even mother Earth may die; it's just nature. So it's okay to also just take a moment and let go of our judgments about our behaviors and start loving ourselves.

Just saying I love myself won't always help solve your problem...

I think we need to understand that loving oneself does not mean pity oneself. I once set up a conference called "Epic Failure Conference," which shows my obsession with failure. I let failure mean a lot. Along the way, I have somehow understood that failure is something I can learn from. There's no such thing as failure. Something happened, and something was missing. This framework of mindset is important because it helps us understand even if we were Michael Jordan, one of the best basketball players in the world, there is still something missing. So even when we succeed, there is still something we can learn.

There is no limit to how much you can love, there is no limit to expansion. Conversely, there is a limit to shrinkage. That limit is called suicide. When people put just too much emphasis on their failures, they shrink and shrink into their suffering. When you can embrace everything around you, even your own shrinking, then there is no stagnation or limitation to expansion.

So what if I just took a stone, threw it into your face, and then I said "Oh, it just happened." That wouldn't be helpful for our societal well-being, would it? What's your take on responsibility?

You took an action, and there is a consequence of this action. It's nobody's fault; actions and their consequences are just facts. That's just what it is, a consequence, and we need to learn how to exist with it. I see failure as something missing in my performance. And my performance is something I can change. When things didn't happen as I expected them to happen — what are the things I can put in place for next time? Which actions can I take to get the result I wanted?

With this mindset, I can feel okay to be responsible for Donald Trump, it just happened and maybe there was something missing that I could do next time to have a different outcome. Taking the freedom to be 100 percent responsible for your actions is empowering. It's just a matter of perspective. Just take a look at your door: It will only open if you get up and go open it. You can't open it by thinking about it. You could wait for somebody to open it for you, but you don't know how long you will need to wait and you are taking the risk that it may never happen. If you choose to get up to open the door, you may fall along the way. Maybe because you forgot to remove a cable on the floor and tripped. What happened was that some action — removing the cable — was missing. It's not rocket science.

In general, within A/E/T, technology is more a technique, something like a tool or a method to help us become who we want to be. Many people believe there is someone who will bring fire to humankind, thinking that once we find the right app, all our problems will be solved, and once bitcoin is stable, it will save us from whatever. I think it's dangerous, to believe in this type of technocracy or techno-solutionism. It's the myth of Prometheus, and it takes us away from our responsibility to be involved in politics.

Then, on the other extreme, there is this myth of Frankenstein, where people are scared that AI will overtake us. I guess the truth is somewhere in between. For instance, when we created the first nuclear weapons, and then we realized we had developed a tool that could destroy all of us, we were shocked. And still, we haven't learned from it, we are doing the same over and over again. We believe we can invent technology that will solve climate change. But technology can't solve climate change for us — it's merely a technique. Basically, we need to learn to tap into our consciousness, and technology is not a shortcut to consciousness. We are creators of technology, and so technology is in its nature a reflection of our actions. The question is: in what state of being are we, while we create this technology? Are we good citizens, wise citizens? We can't outsource humanity to robots!

Any wisdom you want to share with us?

Leadership to me means making things happen that would not have happened otherwise. It means taking action. You can't ask others to do something that you wouldn't do yourself. And I hope that through my sharings, I can inspire others to go in search of their own possibilities. I shared a lot about my individual story and my actions because for me it's important to walk the talk and lead my own life.

In my work with children, I try to ask my kids to heal their relationships with others. I ask them to talk to their friends or family members that they had conflicts with for things as simple as not having washed their dishes. Little things can appear very big sometimes. Or there are kids that don't like to speak in public and I ask them to be courageous. Of course, I'm only a credible teacher when I engage in courageous action myself. Wishful thinking in my own life won't cut it. Ideas are cheap, but actions are the access to transformation. We might not always get what we wanted. What is crucial is to be committed to the future you want to create.

When I also show my vulnerabilities to the kids, I become equal to them. They see my struggle. I speak about my feelings, and we all share our experiences with our individual journeys. I'm just a normal girl, and if I can do it, you can do it too — literally, any human being can do it. My heart just melts when I watch children overcome their fears because they are the next generation of leaders. My life is in their hands, and when I know that they have learned how to be courageous, I know that my life is in good hands.

This is what I keep on seeing in the case of my father and my brother. I know that my father longs for his son. Three and a half years ago, my father wrote a letter, and my brother didn't answer. Then my father had a stroke, and he said: "I just give up on life. I'm waiting to die." In French, there is a saying that says "tant qu'il y a de la vie, il ya de l'espoir" which means "where there's life, there's hope." And I told him, "Your life is only over when you are buried under the ground. But as long as you're still here, you can go on this journey to connect with him." I think he got the message. We both know it's not an easy journey, and we still don't know how this journey will end. But as long as we keep trying, he still has a chance. Just don't wait. There is no someday, there is only one day. And that one day can be today.

Beautiful brains change tomorrow...today
Brain-brush reflection exercise:

How did I feel when I read this?

What did I learn?

What will I integrate into my daily life?

Why don't we brush our brains in the way we brush our teeth?

Philipp Heiler,
founder at brainboost

What topic is most important to your life right now?

I care a lot about mental fitness, mental health and learning. Ever since I was a child, I have spent so much time reflecting on the learning process itself. I asked myself questions like, "How did I learn this information?" or "What is happening with the information in my brain?" I love finding out how to learn things in the shortest amount of time possible. One of the helpful skills for learning new things is the ability to regulate your emotions. In my medical practice, I work with many young patients that suffer from ADD (attention deficit disorder), and this work made me reflect a lot on my own childhood. Many times in school, I already had an answer in my head to whatever the teachers asked. I would yell out the answer as soon as it came to my head. I had this intuition that I would have a much better life if I learned how to gain better self-control and reduce my impulsive behaviors. So I started a self-learning journey to tweak my behavior. I searched for patterns in my decision-making processes. I love harmony and love to have happy people around me, so I have this tendency to avoid conflicts, in particular, social conflicts. And what I tried to understand was: "Why are people reacting in such different ways?" For example, when I compared my reactions to situations that looked similar, I could see that I didn't get angry, whereas other members of my family would get angry quickly. I asked myself, "Why did I not get angry; where is the difference?" I believe the most difficult and yet most important question still to be solved is: "What makes the brain unique?" Let's take two identical twins. They have the same DNA for their brains, and so their brain looks the same, but they are not the same person! Just a split-second after they are born, or even in the womb, they start to become different people, even when they have the same DNA and therefore the same plan for their brains. This is where my fascination for learning and the brain began, and it has been my favorite topic ever since.

What is the current standing in brain research?

The brain is the most important and most complex organ of the human body. It's a big network that has organically grown over decades of life. Over the last few hundred years we have learned a lot about the anatomy of the brain. For the past decades, we have been able to help people with damaged tissues live normal lives thanks to organ transplants. I'm not saying it won't ever be possible to do so with the brain, but from a technical view that would be the most challenging accomplishment. The brain is a network of cells that are linked with cables that look like white mass. We understand roughly how the networks in these brain regions are operating, but actually, we do not know how information flows on the underlying levels. We only have some clues and can derive certain assumptions from the different activity patterns in different parts of the brain. We make these conclusions based on broad brain regions. We haven't yet found a way to measure this. It's maybe comparable to artificial intelligence and machine learning. For example, if you show pictures of men and women to an algorithm, after some time of learning, this algorithm can maybe with ninety-nine percent accuracy tell you the gender of a person. We do not instantly understand the decision-making process of the algorithm. To find out how the algorithm got to this answer, we need to reverse-engineer it because the algorithm grew by itself and was not engineered from an exhaustive pre-defined set of rules. It takes an extra step to identify the patterns that the algorithm used to decide whether this was a man or a woman. We still need to find out how these patterns are induced in human brains at an individual cell level to understand where the differences in certain brain patterns stem from. We need to look deeper into how the network is growing and how the individual parts are interacting in this network.

We know what a brain cell looks like and what type of receptors it has attached to it or what is inside the cell. The brain cells use integrational signals to communicate. Some cables are long, and they end, for example, in your hand. So when you want to move your hand, the information is transmitted from the brain cell to your fingers by this cable. To put it simply, each brain cell has at least a cable attached to it that ends in an organ, a muscle, or another brain cell. During our life, the structure of these networks is constantly changing. In neuroscience, we call this concept neuroplasticity. It means our brains are constantly changing throughout our entire lives. We never stop changing, and we never stop learning. These changes can impact our skills and our well-being. Sometimes we gain happiness, sometimes we lose happiness. Sometimes we learn skills, sometimes we unlearn them. We also know that there are some mental conditions that damage the brain, including Alzheimer's or Parkinson's. Just like with other organs, there are specific problems that can occur in the brain. Some are caused by bacteria, others appear to be caused by autoimmune processes.

Research in the medical field has focused on finding out how to fix problems in a mechanical way. For example, what do we do when a cable in our brain is broken, or how do we remove a tumor without destroying too many parts of the brain. When there is a functional impairment, the most common approach is to provide medication that interacts with certain brain cells in a chemical way. Changes in the brain chemistry influence certain brain activity patterns and can thereby affect the way we feel or how our body behaves. For example, it can affect how quickly we fall asleep. We can also change the function of the brain by coaching therapy. In this approach, we expect the brain will show functional and structural changes when we use it in a different way. In other words, we expect this will lead to the formation of more and different cables. If for example, some lobes in the liver don't work properly, it doesn't matter — maybe the total performance delivery has decreased from one hundred percent to ninety-five percent but this doesn't affect your well-being. In the brain, however, even one single new connection — even though that is very unlikely — could turn you into a different person!

As of today, we don't know exactly what happens when we lose one brain cell. Does it mean that you lose one fraction of your memory, or you lose one skill or would it maybe result in you not being able to recognize one person any more. Probably not, otherwise this would happen all the time. But where is the cutoff? This is what I find so exciting about the research. On a scale from zero to a hundred percent, I'd say we are somewhere at around twenty-five to thirty percent of possible knowledge in understanding our brains. I think we need two things to leap forward: more advanced technology and cross-disciplinary research. There are companies that are currently developing enhanced measurement sensors using quantum technology. They believe they can increase the resolution of the brain signals by 1,000 times. This means instead of measuring activities in brain clusters that contain 100,000,000 brain cells, we could zoom into the workings of 100,000 brain cells or even fewer. We can then analyze the dynamics within more granular micro-structures of the brain. Unfortunately, this technology is still a few years from being market ready. While psychologists or social scientists have already produced great insights about behavioral patterns, like why are certain people more at risk for gambling and how would addiction to gambling compare to addiction to social media, we do not yet have a holistic understanding of the root causes that trigger our behaviors. And then we'd need to understand and integrate findings from neuro-chemicals research as well. How is the blood flow in the brain regulated and which chemicals have which function within the brain network? It's not that we don't have any of this knowledge at all; it's just not yet well integrated.

How do you apply learnings from neuroscience into your everyday life?

In 11th grade, I went to the US for a one-year student exchange. I was a sixteen-year-old boy by that time, and I had been lacking social acceptance, which is, as I mentioned earlier, a key driver of happiness for me. All of a sudden, I was in a new environment, where nobody knew about my past history. This was my once in a lifetime opportunity to try out new behaviors and to act differently than in Germany. I tried different ways of talking to people, different ways of dressing myself. I took new courses in school, tried some new hobbies, and so on. Germany was something exotic to my classmates, and they were so curious to learn more about me. I think this was crucial for me to gain some self-confidence. So I just was more at ease with myself. And this killed the need for overthinking about how to present myself to others and about how they would react. When I stopped thinking all the time about what others would think, I could pay more attention to them, start to listen to them, and show some empathy. I think one of the major drivers was that I stopped thinking that people wanted to attack me when they said something. Simple self-awareness helped me interpret things other people said in a different way. So for me, it took one year being somewhere else and then coming back to re-enter my social group with an updated version of myself. I was more mindful and more aware of human interaction. In retrospect, I still had a long way to go, but this was a huge boost to my personal well-being at that time.

During med school, my brother and I came across this technology called neurofeedback, where you use a brain computer interface to mirror back to a person what is happening inside the brain by measuring brain activity. With current brain measurement technologies, we can measure different mental states of the brain during different daily activities, as in what happens while we work, while we relax, while we sleep, and so on. We can from this basic pool of information quickly derive what our brain needs most to work in a natural way. Neurofeedback is built on the understanding that we can help the brain transform by providing close to real-time feedback loops. We look for an abnormal brain activity pattern that creates a problem, for example, leading to depressive feelings, and we try to become aware of it. Then we can find ways to influence it in a way that helps us improve the quality of life. We were so fascinated by the opportunities to help people improve their well-being that we created a company offering neurofeedback therapy and training for individuals and corporations.

What does decision-making in a neuroscience based company look like?

In our company, we don't do year-end performance reviews, we do frequent regular feedback rounds, where we focus on appreciation and lessons learned. We try to create an environment with friendly vibes, an environment that feels safe to our team members, so that they do not need to be scared. We do not yell at our employees, or I would not ask team members to report to me why they failed in front of the entire team. I have always wanted to create meaning in our work, not only for me, but also for others. Social recognition is a big motivator for me, and it means a lot to me when people say, "Hey Philipp, thank you for helping me to do this or that," or when they tell me that I have created something meaningful for their lives. At this point in my life, this is more important to me than having a high salary. Brainboost as a company is vision-drivin and not so much profit-driven. We try to live by that, and I try to base my leadership style on that. I don't want to be the guy who improves himself just for the sake of it, so I try to make feedback a meaningful learning opportunity for all participants. It had happened in the past, that I gave a task to somebody and asked them "Are you okay with this?" and they said yes. It took me some time to understand that they had only said so because they were too scared to say no to their boss, which is not a great ground for learning. This is particularly interesting because I have said many times that it would be no problem to say "no." But only saying the word does not mean that your team will instantly accept this as a fact. They need to experience the situation and your way of handling problems to believe that what you say is true. It is called implicit learning, which means learning based on experiences and situations. This is in my opinion the most important quality of a leader: they need to show the team their leadership style and live it everyday — just telling it is not enough. If a person misses deadlines a few times in a row, then we are looking into identifying and understanding the underlying pattern. It might be as simple as too much noise in the workplace, or it can be a misunderstanding of the task, so I need to communicate clearer. If I ask for a competitor analysis summary, I'm specific in if I'd want something that can be done in two hours, like just a quick Google search, or if they should spend one week on it. Sometimes, a person might not have enough experience to do a task in an efficient way. They may double check results all the time when there is no double checking needed. It may be linked to some type of brain habit or fear pattern which is unhelpful in a given context. Feedback is the starting point for learning. Each interaction is an opportunity to learn and provide guidance if needed. So we sit together and look for this one brain habit pattern, and we try to solve it at its root cause. This speeds up the learning process.

There is one lesson about appreciation that I would like to share with you because it was an eye-opening experience for us. We are a self-funded start-up, and as such, we have to be resourceful with our budget. So typically, we look carefully where we invest our funds to make sure we will make enough returns to re-invest and grow the company. But for our last Christmas party, we decided to buy gift cards of one hundred Euro per employee, which, for a startup like ours, is a significant investment. It meant diverting funds from investments with measurable outcomes like Google advertisements into building intangible assets. The feedback we received was good — the team was happy, and I think, even when you can't measure team happiness in numbers, this was exactly the right decision.

In general, when it comes to decision-making, the first person I consult is myself. If I, for example, make an offer to someone, I always ask myself first: "Would I be accepting this offer myself? What would sound crazy about it? What would be lacking for me? How would the conditions need to change for the offer to be acceptable?" Then we test the idea in our team meetings and gather team member feedback. It's an important sanity check. Oddly enough, even when we do thorough first checks, we find out that we treat others differently to how we'd like to be treated as a customer! It has happened so many times, even when I try to be so conscious about it. When we believe we have an acceptable concept, we test our assumptions with real customers early in the process with prototypes that might not yet have an elaborate user design. In my view, it's more important to have an acceptable product quality, rather than for the product to be perfect. In the end, it's the people from outside the organization that will pay for the product, not our team — so getting honest, real customer feedback early on is important.

How do we keep our brains happy?

First of all, we need to understand that just like any other part of your human body, the brain needs maintenance and attention. From a medical perspective, the brain is the most challenging organ to ever replace in case it is impaired. When other organs don't work, we now have solutions to regrow tissue, supplement the functions with technical machines, or do both. So it's actually worth trying to understand as much as we can about our brain to keep it safe. It is something you will need to live with your entire life. For example, most people brush their teeth at least two times a day. So they invest six minutes daily to care for their teeth. But most people invest zero minutes a day to keep their brains functioning — and I know this is repetitive, but in my view, the brain is the most important organ in our body. So maybe the first step is to just invest at least six minutes a day in taking care of our brain.

The key element to brushing your brain is mindfulness. We need to learn to be aware of our feelings. They are the basic drivers of our behaviors. Mindful brain brushing means to know how it feels when our brain is generating brain wave activities that we consider "healthy." In this way, we can start engaging with our mental states and create more helpful brain activity patterns. What typically happens in a stressful situation is that people want to leave the negative situation, but they do not know where to go. Or when they want to sleep, they don't know what to do. They keep saying to themselves: "I need to sleep; I need to relax; I need to sleep." This creates stress, and maybe even anxiety. The problem is: To relax, I need to let go of these anxious thoughts. In a stressful situation, I just go to a safe space in my head so that I don't need to run into this anxious pattern. To get to this safe space, I use a relaxation technique called "Autogenic Training." I learned it as a kid because I had difficulties sleeping. I know exactly what my safe space looks like because, in my mind, I have gone there many times. It's the place where, over many years, I have coped with many challenging situations and worked with uncomfortable emotions. I have linked many positive experiences to that place. It's comparable to meditation. When you lose your focus, you just bring it back to your breathing and you do that over and over again. So when I get too stressed, I escape, replenish my mental resources, and sit with the anxiety until I'm ready to come back. An important part of this technique is habit and repetition. The safe space has to grow over time and be established in the brain so strongly that it is a reliable place to go even in stressful situations.

Learning about things that matter to you in a way that matters to you is another way of brain brushing. I have to admit I don't like to read books, but I like to read articles that portray the newest innovations in technology. I have cleaned my social media feeds from all the unnecessary clutter and now I use my LinkedIn feed as my personalized news portal. I follow the activities of people I find interesting. This has two benefits. One is, I always get the newest updates on topics that I care about. Second, it's just cool to discover the world from the eyes of the people that I choose to follow.

So to put it in a nutshell: First, give your brain some space and time to figure things out. Understand what is going on inside yourself first in terms of: How does this make me feel? What would I call this emotional reaction? Then find your personal way of brain brushing — it's different for each person and each situation.

How would the world appear if we understood as much as we could about the brain?

One use case is education. We already know that some children learn faster with pictures, while others need auditive input to process information and so on. We will get to a state where we have customized content for school children with their general and current brain activity patterns. This holds true for adult education — and I think we need this if we want to realize life-long learning. If we collect more data on our brains, we can learn more about our brain patterns and derive ways to better learn. There are so many positive effects and new opportunities that we might not even think of today that help us understand how to increase well-being for human beings. I could imagine we develop something like a brain database in the next ten to fifteen years that enables us to understand ourselves better. In my view, in particular for children, knowing how the individual brain works is a big lever for improving quality of life. If we had a universal database, we could know what type of eating habits or education system, what type of physical training is most favorable to support a child's development and its well-being.

On the other end, we also need to understand in which ways we damage our brains. Sometimes we engage in leisure activities that are not helpful for our well-being, like excess TV or social media consumption. And it doesn't stop on the individual level. We also need to examine negative external effects of harmful behavior for the entire society. Let me give you an example: In social media, it's easy to insult someone by posting an offensive comment. It's easier than saying it to someone's face. However, the person who reads this comment may suffer as much from reading this comment as if it had happened in person; and when this is multiplied, we create these grand emotional imbalances. What I'm trying to say is we need to understand better how technological innovation influences our brains, so that we can create guidelines for behavior that does not harm the well-being of entire societies.

Any other thoughts that you want to share with us?

Many people believe we need willpower to change something in our brain. But this is only part of the equation. What we actually need is a lot of exercising. The brain is also just an organ, and like other organs, it needs training. If I decide I want to stay calmer or that I want to sleep better, it will not happen overnight. I can't decide to just raise my pulse or make my muscles grow overnight. Our physiology only changes if we do something regularly. Unfortunately, we cannot install a mental change program and see instant progress. It is not only important that you actively make a decision to change something; it is equally important that you set up a process to stick with your plan for a certain time.

When it comes to technology, I do hope that people do not get scared away from all the possibilities of advancement. Every piece of information can be used in a helpful or harmful way. We need to develop this moral compass, just as in other fields that are working with sensitive information. Until then, I hope that companies, governments, insurance companies, and so on do not misuse the data to fuel people's fears. Hopefully, we can develop a global consent toward how to deal with brain data as with other sensitive information. Finally, I believe that societal demand plays a big role — once society has understood the importance of brain research for our well-being, there will be more funding available for research. This demand will help craft a bigger picture of what the brain, what mental health, or even mental fitness means for humanity.

Beautiful brains change tomorrow...today
Brain-brush reflection exercise:

How did I feel when I read this?

What did I learn?

What will I integrate into my daily life?

Make happiness work for positive change

Dr. Kerstin Humberg,
founder of Yunel

How do you currently spend most of your working life, what are you excited about?

I am passionate about two topics: positive psychology and social entrepreneurship. Already in high school, I was fascinated by human development: how we as Homo sapiens learn, how we unleash our potential, and how we shape our planet. That's the reason I chose to study human geography, political sciences, and psychology. Later, back in 2008, while working at McKinsey, I decided to focus my PhD research on poverty reduction through social business in Bangladesh. Ever since, Nobel Peace Laureate Muhammad Yunus has been an amazing source of inspiration for me. Today, I combine both topics through my work with Yunel.

What does Yunel do?

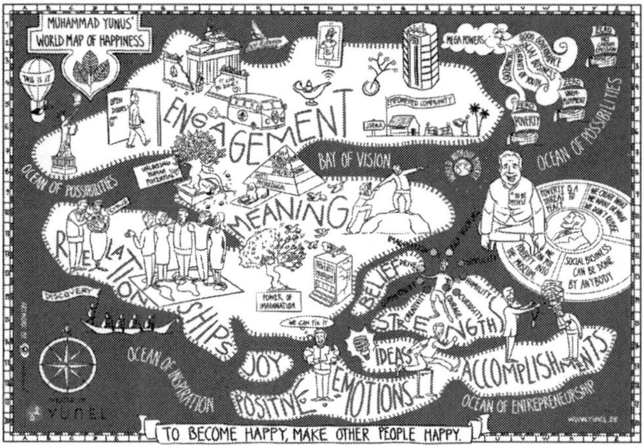

Yunel offers a novel approach to leadership development and life strategy for executives, social innovators, and entrepreneurs based on positive psychology. We help clients treasure significant life experiences, embrace the art and science of happiness, and prepare themselves for a future with purpose and impact. We jointly explore what makes their lives most worth living and develop an inspiring vision for the years to come. Visualization is a key component of our work because research in positive psychology and neuroscience has proved the power of images in changing human mindsets and behavior. Our products comprise illustrated "halftime" biographies in book format, vision posters, and beautiful life maps. In addition to our work with private individuals, we offer tailored programs for corporate and non-profit organizations, e.g. training, workshops, and leadership retreats.

Where and how did you stumble upon positive psychology in the first place?

In 2013, I met Harvard professor Tal-Ben Shahar. During one of McKinsey's professional programs, he delivered a keynote speech on happiness. I was thrilled. Tal-Ben Shahar spoke about the factors which help children flourish. Suddenly, I realized that my parents had passed the test. They probably had never heard of positive psychology but provided an environment in which my brothers and I could thrive. They offered unconditional love, nurtured our strengths, and encouraged us to volunteer our time for social and environmental causes. Every night, they prayed with us and, thereby, cultivated a strong sense of gratitude for what we had. The more I read about the science of happiness and well-being, the more I felt that positive psychology was the ultimate key to starting my own mission-driven enterprise. In 2014, I quit my job with McKinsey and started "Yunel," a company with a mission to unleash human potential and happiness for positive social change. In short, to make happiness work. Why? Simply because happy people are more collaborative, creative, and altruistic — to name just a few positive characteristics.

What is positive psychology about?

Positive psychology can be described as the science of happiness and well-being; it seeks to identify what makes healthy people thrive. What does it take to be happy and which factors affect sustained psychological well-being? What makes human life most worth living? Christopher Peterson, a pioneer in positive psychology research, once described the field in one sentence by saying "other people matter." Although he admitted that this might sound like a bumper sticker slogan, it was in fact the essence of what positive psychology research has shown about a life well-lived. Ultimately, human beings thrive on social connection and love.

What's the difference between happiness and well-being?

Happiness can be described as subjective well-being. It depends on two components: emotions and life satisfaction. It captures how frequently we experience positive versus negative emotions and the level of satisfaction with our personal lives. The good news: for our subjective well-being, personal mindsets and behaviors are considered as more influential than external life conditions. Therefore, happiness can be increased, e.g., through focused awareness or the cultivation of positive emotions such as joy, gratitude, or love. By now, most research in positive psychology has a focus on psychological well-being. Martin Seligman, a former president of the American Psychological Association and so-called father of the domain, describes psychological well-being as made up of five pillars: Positive emotions, Engagement, Relationships, Meaning, and Accomplishment (PERMA). His model is a scientific theory that goes beyond happiness. PERMA implies positive effects on performance, creativity, social relationships, and the motivation to pursue new goals.

How scientifically proven are the insights from this field?

Positive psychology is an academic field. It is based on research. That's the beauty of it in contrast to so many self-help books that rely on personal stories and case studies. To give an example: in her broaden-and-build theory, Barbara Fredrickson has investigated how positive emotions like joy, inspiration, and love affect our brain. Positive emotions literally expand our horizons and prepare the ground for personal development and growth. Fredrickson's work is an important cornerstone in advancing our understanding of human well-being. Another pioneer is Shawn Achor, author of *Big Potential* and *The Happiness Advantage*. According to Achor, we should actively invest in our happiness and well-being because happiness drives performance and success — not the other way round. Achor illustrates how waiting to be happy actually limits our brain's potential for success, whereas cultivating positive brains makes us more creative, motivated, productive, and resilient which drives performance upward. In a positive state, our brains simply function better than in neutral or negative states.

Tell us a bit more about Yunel. How did Yunel come about?

Looking back, I believe the seed was planted more than twenty years ago. At the age of twenty-one, I had completed my journalism education and was working for the German Press Agency in South Africa. Coming from a peaceful village in western Germany, I was shocked to find myself confronted with HIV, racism, and crime. After two months, I was attacked on a public train. My friend Thorsten and I were surrounded by five armed men and, for a few minutes, I thought: that's it. Game over. Even worse: the train was full of people, but no one came to our aid. What a traumatic experience! Ever since, I have wondered: what holds us back from helping one another? Why do we tolerate so much social injustice in the world and what can we do about it? In consequence, I focused my university studies on development topics, looking into education, health, and development policies for the well-being of societies. Over time, I became more and more disillusioned. I realized that traditional development aid is not the solution. In 2006, I decided to join McKinsey & Company to explore the role of the private sector in shaping our common future. After nine years, mostly with McKinsey's Sustainability & Resource Productivity Practice, I felt there was a more creative way for me to unleash my potential. Inspired by positive psychology, I founded Yunel to further align my personal values, professional objectives, and skills. The name Yunel pays tribute to Nobel Peace Laureates Muhammad Yunus from Bangladesh and Nelson Mandela from South Africa as leading examples of human potential realized against all odds. Both of them have shown what individuals can achieve if they combine a strong vision with passion and perseverance. We can all transform entire societies for the better!

How can one find purpose and meaning in life?

It's a journey. It has been said that the two most important days in your life are the day you are born and the day you find out why. Finding purpose and meaning typically requires exploration. In the external world as well as internally through introspection and reflection. Austrian neurologist and psychiatrist Viktor Frankl described the pursuit of meaning as man's primary motivational force. In fact, as long as human beings have been around, they have questioned the reason for their existence. Aristotle spent his lifetime reflecting on this and concluded that the ultimate purpose in life was to be happy. However, in my view, happiness is not a goal in itself, rather a byproduct. Personally, I regard happiness as the joy and inspiration we feel striving to achieve our potential and the belief that change is possible. We can find purpose and meaning if we explore our values, follow our passions, build on our signature strengths, discover what the world needs, and try to make a positive difference. According to Frankl, a meaningful life consists of many meaningful moments and meaning can be discovered at any time. We can always choose our inner attitude in response to external experiences.

What's your purpose in life and how did you find it?

"To make happiness work." Maybe this will change over time, but that's okay. When I reflect on my past, I realize how the attack in South Africa pushed me out of my comfort zone. The experience, traumatic in nature, raised fundamental questions that I had to explore. All over the world. Looking back, the attack and my perceived helplessness was a meaningful experience. Although very difficult to deal with at first, it put me on an exciting path. In search of meaning, I chose very different careers. I went from journalism to development collaboration and from there to management consultancy. Today, when I work with my clients at Yunel, I draw from all my previous professional experiences and networks. It seems as if this journey of discovery was necessary for me to create Yunel.

What changes when you have found your purpose and commit to it?

You get more of a sparkle in your eyes. I have certainly become more centered since I founded Yunel. When you focus on what really matters to you, other things start falling into place as well. However, sometimes, purpose-driven endeavors can also feel like a burden. There seems to be no way out.

How do you deal with challenges?

I struggle. Like most people do. We like to assume that normally everything goes well, but that's not the case. Life is full of ups and downs. That's a given and, in this context, I would like to emphasize that positive psychology is not a "happyology." While the first wave of research in positive psychology has had a strong focus on happiness and the role of positive emotions, we currently see a growing interest in negative emotions or "the upside of our dark side," respectively. Crises or losses often create pain and suffering because they relate to something that once contributed to positive experiences in our life. Why do we suffer when we lose a person? Most likely because we felt love for that person. Both positive and negative emotions are part of our lives, and we need to deal with them. Feelings like anger, guilt, or anxiety may be uncomfortable, but they are also incredibly useful. Anger fuels creativity, guilt may spark improvement, and self-doubt can enhance performance. In order to flourish, we need to cultivate our emotional agility, the ability to access our full range of emotions, not just the good ones.

How do you do that?

Daily meditation and gratitude practices help me deal with those emotions. Every night, before I go to sleep, I count my blessings. A challenge in today's world is that our brains seem to overreact to potential risks. Our "catastrophic brain" reacts to little triggers, such as another human being frowning, as if they were big threats, as if we were facing a dangerous animal in the wild. This phenomenon consumes a lot of energy and brain capacity. Therefore, it's crucial to understand how emotions affect our capacity to think, and how we can learn to tolerate pain in a helpful rather than harmful way. Ray Dalio, a successful American investor, recently published a book called *Principles*, where he came up with the following formula: "Pain plus reflection equals progress." What a great way to frame this!

How do your clients react to these kinds of insights?

When working towards building meaning in life, I sometimes ask my clients: if today your doctor told you that you only had three more months to live, how would you spend them? To see how people react is quite revealing. Some say, I would change nothing. Others say, I would make sure that I complete the task at hand and ensure a proper handover before I go on a final vacation. And others say, I would immediately drop the ball and do something completely different. When I have clients from the latter category, I ask them: why don't you do that now because your life could be over tomorrow? If we don't start enacting a meaningful life today, it might be too late! Our life is finite and this fact is extremely powerful. If we were to live forever, there would be no reason to live a meaningful life today. Seeing your life from this perspective might cause a little bit of suffering at first, but I think the sooner we understand what we are missing out on, the earlier we can start to make a change. Even small steps in the desired direction can give us a sense of self-efficacy and fuel our motivation to take bolder steps along the way.

How do you deal with weaknesses?

I try to accept them. In general, I prefer to build on my strengths. In this context, positive psychologists like to use the metaphor of a sailing boat. Weaknesses are described as little holes in the bottom of the boat. Of course, we need to make sure that they don't endanger our lives, but the sails are our strengths. The more wisely we use our strengths and align them to the wind, the more easily we can move toward our destiny. The more we know and build on our strengths, the bigger the sail and the more wind can push you into the direction you want to go. In my view, it's more important to identify and cultivate our strengths than trying to fix minor weaknesses. To illustrate this perspective, medical doctor and author Eckart von Hirschhausen refers to a penguin. At first glance, the penguin looks like a pretty poor creature. It doesn't have any knees and it cannot walk very quickly. But once the penguin is in the water, it becomes hyper-efficient. The moral of the story: context matters as well. As penguins, we'd do better to put ourselves into the water and not into the desert because even ten years of psychotherapy won't make a penguin a camel!

How do I influence my well-being?

Invest in your PERMA. Start to meditate. Ten minutes per day already makes a huge difference and positively affects parts of our brain that are responsible for self-awareness, concentration, and learning. Actively cultivate positive emotions. For example, by "counting your blessings" or identifying "three good things" every day. These are easy and well-proven techniques. To prepare for a good tomorrow, ask yourself: what three things were good today? What did I enjoy? For each of these three good things, then investigate: what was my contribution to make it happen? This reflection positively affects our sleep and sharpens our awareness of all the good things in everyday life that our "catastrophic brain" doesn't appreciate enough. Spend time with people close to your heart. Listen to them. Make them happy. You also could explore your signature strengths. What were the activities you enjoyed as a child? Today, what kind of activities put you into a flow state? When do you lose your sense of space and time? Signature strengths boost your energy when you use them; they are what you believe has always been true about you. If you want to build on them, you've got to know them and also value and accept them.

You have an open stage to share whatever is top of your heart with the readers:

What's the essence of being human? Over time, I have come to the conclusion that there are at least three elements: one is the ability to love, which prepares the ground for social connection. Second, we are able to collaborate in large groups and on a global scale. Third, the power of imagination. We can envision a future that we would like to live in and anchor its picture in our mind. This picture can become reality if we nourish our ability to love and collaborate. Together, we can get there.

Beautiful brains change tomorrow...today
Brain-brush reflection exercise:

How did I feel when I read this?

What did I learn?

What will I integrate into my daily life?

Level up your game: from Mindmastery to Soulmastery

Julia Merkt and Michael Lubomirski, founders of Soulmastery and Soulartist

Let's take a moment to reflect on what is actually important to you right now.

Michael: We have discovered, through our meditation practices, that the realm of material things is something like a Penrose staircase. You have the feeling you're climbing the ladder, but in the end, you are remaining at the same point where you started off. In this material realm, we tend to run after material things. We even treat other human beings as goods. You can only break through this vicious circle when you stop and understand that the present moment is what matters, not the future ladder. We have gone through evolutions, both in our personal and professional lives, and we have created our company Soulmastery to combine both personal growth as our personal purpose with a way to earn a living. It's integrated. Our business is to share our learnings, our tools and experiences with other people, so whoever wants to start a personal transformation can just learn how to do it.

Personal transformation is a process and there are certain methods that help you on the way. Let's say, it's like the car, that helps you travel on your journey. We have discovered and developed very powerful meditation techniques and are constantly learning new ones and shaping existing ones, so that we can share them with others. We called our company Soulmastery because the mind is a beautiful tool that we've been given by God, the universe, you can call it whatever — existence, Buddha, Christ, whatever resonates with you. It's a brilliant tool. It's maybe the most evolved tool in the universe, right? It can think, analyze, memorize, produce feelings, do all kinds of stuff. The sciences can tell you what the brain does and to an extent how it works, but they do not really explain why there is a brain. Our experience is that through meditation, we can transfer the mastery of our being from the monopoly of the mind, towards a unity of mind, body, and soul.

The concept of soul is maybe a little bit mystical to start out with. What we mean by soul, is that there is something like a spark, something inside us, that makes us whole. You cannot find it when you dissect the body. Some people have said that the body becomes twelve grams lighter after we die. What is it, that vanishes, after we leave our body? Some people call this spirit, others call it heart. We call it soul, and we think that it's our real inner master. The mind is not a good master because it is wild, it can be schizophrenic, it sometimes makes us happy in the morning and sad in the evening. One morning you love a person, in the evening you hate the person. It's not very consistent. In our view, the mind is a muscle, maybe something like a bicep. Just imagine you flex your bicep for an entire day — it will be very tired, and it will change its nature, its form. With our mind, it's the same. If we use it all the time, it gets tired. If we let it rest, it becomes so much more powerful when we need it.

What are these meditation techniques?

Julia: Meditation is the contemplation of the interaction between our unconscious and our conscious. Today, many people are very busy, and they are in activity mode throughout the entire day. Asking someone to just sit down and observe their mind is very difficult. For many beginners, the moment they close their eyes, instead of enjoying calm, they feel their inner chatter starting, and many unpleasant thoughts pop up. It makes it very difficult to sit still and bring up the calmness to observe what is happening inside you. So what we do is facilitate a smooth transition into silence through activity. The methods we use are mostly active meditations (OSHO Active Meditations™). They last around one hour and contain several stages of activity, of which some stages contain physical activity, such as laughter, crying, jumping, humming, before you get into the silent part of the meditation. We use the active part of the meditation to help with the catharsis, the letting go or expressing whatever is stored underneath the daily noise in our systems, to tap into the undercurrents. So we release the tension that has built up during the day, by giving it a space to come out, and then we are ready to dive into silence.

For beginners of meditation practice, and for busy people in general, it's a very effective way to help you get in touch with the power of silence, of stillness of the mind. For many people, it's a real aha-moment, when they for the first time in their lives consciously experience some seconds of peaceful silence in their heads. Once you have had this experience, then you don't need to believe in the power of meditation anymore. Your brain knows that it exists, and you have a foundation — an experience — upon which to build.

Silence is so important in our world, which is full of noise, wherever we go. In silence, you can actually touch the essence of your being. You can just be free from this noise, not thinking, and then you can try to play a little bit with this new freedom. People typically describe it as a life-changing experience!

In which way is silence a life-changing experience?

Julia: For me, learning to cultivate this inner silence through the meditations has helped me to tap into my creativity. When I meditate, I watch myself, I'm a witness to my own consciousness. I watch myself in a curious way, not in a judgmental way. There is no good or bad, just watching and I begin to understand what drives me. If there's a an emotional wound you want to leave behind, then spend time observing it. The more you observe, the closer you come to transcending and leaving it behind. Active meditation is quite a fun and relaxing activity; it has a very playful character. It helps us get in touch with our inner child again. It's a very blissful experience, to understand yourself a little bit better, feel your passions. I worked in a bank before I started with meditation. And now I'm an artist. I had never thought about painting or writing books before, but now I do both. So ultimately, it's about becoming the master of my own being. This gives me freedom to decide what I want to do. This freedom gives me an inner state of bliss. That is much more than just being happy. It's being content with life because I simply am. Self-development is not like finding an end to something. It's more about enjoying the path, and it's about enjoying every moment of your life. I think through the process of meditation, if you come more and more into your heart, you can find the purpose in your life because it's inside you. Everyone has a seed inside of them, and they need to cultivate that seed. When we grow these seeds, our skills grow, and our passions might evolve.. Most important is that we act on our purpose, from our heart, from our soul!

Michael: For me, learning how to meditate has changed my perspective on the purpose of my life. I'm an immigrant from Russia. I came to Germany as a kid. My life was very focused on earning a lot of money, having a great career, driving a nice car. So I owned many things, but I was not in the driver's seat of my own life! I was driven by the wants and needs of other people in my ecosystem, and there is nothing bad about fulfilling these needs as long as you do it consciously. For me, it was more an unconscious driver of my life decisions. I thought that I was acting on my own values, and that these values were super important. When I learned to stop seeking for material growth and question whether all these values that I had enacted were my own values, I discovered they were the values of my ecosystem, installed into my unconscious. They had been there for thirty-five years.

There are many good philosophical scriptures on the topic, but then we are not philosophers. What I can say is that I have experienced the fact that we all shape our own reality. Our thoughts shape our attitude, and our attitude matters because it guides our actions. When you have crazy thoughts, and your brain is looping back and forth, how can you switch off. You start to have the same thoughts over and over again, you start to create decision trees for whatever might happen next. These mind games are exhausting. When you start meditating, you can leave the future and come back to the here and now. I'm not saying let's stop all planning and let's go to the casino, put everything on the line, lose everything and be happy and dance in the rain. We still have a life to live; we have basic needs; but we can keep the planning and the worrying to what is necessary in the moment.

I have discovered that most of the joy that I experienced in earlier days was linked to future projections. I looked forward to my next holiday, and so I started to spend time planning to book the best hotel resort to relax. And when the holiday was nearing the end, I felt very sad, and already thought about the next holiday, sometimes even starting from the first day into the vacation. I was always living in the future! I did not have the time to enjoy what I had already achieved, or what was happening around me, but was rather thinking about the new car, the new watch, and so on. I was never in the present moment to enjoy the beauty of my life and my being, because I was so driven by materialism. It's amazing how the mind just masters my thinking, when I'm letting it run wild. I grew up in Moscow, and there were many times when there was nothing to buy in the grocery stores. In the western world, most of our basic needs are fulfilled, and I didn't know how to appreciate it. I didn't care that the sun was shining, or that I was sitting in a wonderful chair. Drawing joy from future expectations is also very dangerous because the future is a moving target. You can start imagining something and once you come close to its realization, it's already moving. A disappointment is bound to follow most future projections.

When we started with personal transformation, we learned about consciousness, mindfulness, meditation. It's about zooming out from the current surroundings and having a more holistic perspective on myself and my position in the universe. That's a completely different sense of purpose. I discovered that all the material things I had been running after were actually egocentric things, and it's a bit senseless, because the world does not revolve around myself. When you can bring your happiness to the present moment, you start shaping your own reality to become blissful. When you know yourself, things change, because you understand how you want to live your life. That's the life-changing part of it. I realized what it was that I really needed in order to live a good life. When you know what you want deep down in the core of your essence, then you can make decisions that feel very right because they come from your heart, not from your brain. Now I think that there have been certain skills and talents that have been given to me, and I think that my purpose is to leverage and use these talents in order to grow and to become more conscious.

How do you master your soul?

Julia: What we train during meditation is to let the mind know that there is another master in the house. And that the mind can relax a little bit, take a rest. Just like muscles need to rest, so they can grow. The next time you need the mind again, it is ready to help you get into flow. Living life requires a lot of creativity, and when our mind is working all the time, it is too tired to perform when we need it. We also think that the soul is the unifying element between mind and body. So if we let the mind go crazy, we might experience problems with our body or our soul because they are out of harmony. Alignment of body, mind, and soul helps us to trust ourselves and our intuition. It helps us come up with the right solution at the right time.

A rested mind can help you tap into your creativity. It does so because it creates space for the soul to take over its mastery role. Unfortunately, it's a slow process. It takes a little bit of meditation experience to reach this flow state on the spot.

Michael: We tend to judge everything, especially people; it just happens automatically. You don't even talk to the person. You don't know them. But you have already judged them. This is how our minds work. What we do in meditation, is try to minimize the delta between the moment we judge and the moment we notice it. In the beginning, you may only notice after maybe half a minute that you have judged another person. If you put enough emphasis on observing yourself passing a judgment, the timeframe between passing the judgment will become shorter and shorter until it's nearly zero. You will notice the feeling of judgment arising in your yourself as soon as you see a person, and this is where change starts to happen. Whenever you start observing yourself in a certain habit, certain way, certain behavior, you can see the pattern of judgment arising, and this is where you can decide to act on it or not — without suppressing or condemning yourself.

Let me make it very practical: you can give yourself the task today to catch yourself judging others. By the end of the day you may already notice a difference. This is where transformation starts. Just by observing your behavior, it might dissolve by itself. No need to bury or suppress it. Just observe, observe, observe, and don't judge yourself. One day you will step outside and realize you have a different outlook. The people are the same, but your perspective has changed. So by simply training your mind, you are shaping your own reality. Observation is so powerful because it makes the unconscious conscious. This is the driver behind psychoanalysis. This is the mentality behind Zen. It's about bringing the unconscious part of our being into our conscious field. By observing the negative attitude, you will soon notice the feeling as it arises. It's just a feeling. It's just a sensation. It's not the thought yet.

So meditation is about becoming happy?

Michael: There's no ultimate goal in meditation. Meditation gives you freedom, freedom from your drivers. So that it's okay to have ups and downs in life, they are like waves, coming, going. You can enjoy riding all these waves. It's not about not caring, it's about being content with these dynamics. It's about understanding that life is more than just happiness, there are highs and lows. Sometimes you're happy, sometimes you're not, that's okay. But you can always appreciate what is happening. So even unhappiness can be appreciated. I use meditation to get to know myself better. Knowing yourself is a great virtue and a noble quest worth pursuing for everybody. To me it feels like a never-ending journey; it's always a work in progress, but it's very exciting. This is about recognizing oneself. We have the impression that we know our purpose in the moment, meaning that we are on the right path, towards Enlightenment, Nirvana, or whatever you want to call the full self-realization, but who would know if this impression is actually right?

What would happen to society if many people discovered their true nature?

Julia: Meditation teaches you to draw joy from even the unhappy moments in life. Because we can train ourselves how to stop judging. And if everybody would meditate, and maybe just designate five percent more of their mind to the here and now, then there is a huge potential for a big societal change. I'm an economist by training, and what I think is that when more people learn to see things from a different perspective, there will be an end to the quest for economic growth. This might require certain systemic changes, and this is a way bigger topic than meditation. I'm not a politician or a philosopher, so I will leave this topic to the experts. It is not my purpose to change the system, but I'm certain that each of us can contribute to this change by changing our own reality. My purpose is to provide a framework to everybody who wants to start this journey, to live a more conscious and more blissful life. Just imagine if all these grim, stressed faces you see in the subway or at work, if they were just five percent happier — imagine how different the world would feel. It would create some spiral dynamics, and advance our entire society.

Please share with us whatever comes up in your hearts.

Michael: I don't know if our being here in this universe is a big joke, a parallel reality, a computer simulation or whatever, but I think that we are here to experience human life as it happens. My aspiration is to experience myself in this realm as purely as possible, so dropping all judgments, all filters, that partially prevent me from having the undistorted experience of what life is and who I am. I think that this experience of being can be enhanced through meditation and awareness. There are so many different forms of meditation. Meditation is free of cost and is available to anyone, anywhere. It's worth trying.

Julia: The invitation to you is, in case you are interested in meditation, go try it. It's not something to speak about; it needs to be experienced.

Beautiful brains change tomorrow...today
Brain-brush reflection exercise:

How did I feel when I read this?

What did I learn?

What will I integrate into my daily life?

Balance as a life philosophy

Karisha Adatia,

PhD student in polymer chemistry and managing director of Akram

What is most important in your life right now?

There are three major topics that are very dear to my heart right now. All three have an impact on both my personal life and also my view on the world. Looking at this world, I think, we are facing three three major crises: a crisis of ecology, a crisis of society where the income gap is growing rapidly, and a crisis of character, in which many people have lost their connection to their inner self.

Even living a quite privileged life in Germany, so many families are struggling to find their balance between work, family, friends, engagement, and simply leading their household. It feels that there is not enough time left to breathe and to live life fully. So many of us are searching for some deeper sense of happiness and meaning. We search for it mostly in the external world, but rarely look for it inside ourselves. I feel a big lack of mindfulness and awareness in our society of today. I feel there is a big need for creating an environment where we don't have to numb our feelings, our sensations, and our intellect to cope with the day. We are neglecting to nurture our soul, which in my eyes is the true source of real happiness.

In my personal life, I am currently figuring out how to make good decisions for my future in a way that I can unfold my potential and at the same time reach a balance that allows the different parts of myself to flourish fully. Since the beginnings of my studies, I have been leading our family business, Akram, and now that I am about to finish my PhD and that the family business has been successfully sold to a new, responsible manager, I am about to decide where my future will lead me and to which company I am going to dedicate myself. There are three questions that I do have in mind when looking at the job market: What is my true ambition? How can I contribute my talents and my personality in order to have a real positive impact? What is it that I want to dedicate myself to, and what is it that truly gives me something back? Coming back to the three crises I see in the world, for me personally, anything which is not focused on solving one of these crises, can't be an option right now.

How do you cope with the crisis of character?

I strongly believe everything is interconnected. As much as it's true that the world will not change dramatically and immediately just because I change something in my life, it is also true that everything we think, say, or do does have consequences – even if we don't experience them straight away. My journey to combat the "crisis of character" in my personal life started with easy and small steps like meditation, yoga, and healthy food. This helps me to be more balanced and to be reconnected to myself. Doing this, I can see more clearly what inspires or motivates me. For example, I have found out that I am often impressed by a certain kind of prestige and – let's call it – by shiny things, that might even glitter a bit. So, job opportunities that promise a certain kind of prestige, do attract me. But in reality, looking for a job is like searching for a pair of trainers to master a challenging hike. And I am asking myself: Do I really want the shiny high heels for this? I believe it is all about compatibility! Do your shoes and the environment you want to have an impact on really fit together? Do I want the hike or a red carpet? These questions are crucial when making your way through the jungle of possibilities. And maybe a humble pair of trainers (possibly with a spark of glitter) might be the better choice for me.

All in all, coping with the crisis of character is a deeply personal thing and no one can find an answer to it but yourself. I believe having the courage to be honest with yourself and focus on what you really want to achieve is a key to mastering it.

How would you find out if you wanted the red carpet or the hike?

That's intuition. I think everybody knows what they really want, if they were just brave enough to admit it. I also know that I want to be a giving person, someone who gives love, who cares and who contributes positively to a community. I want to be a person who has enough time to prepare delicious Indian meals for family and friends or take the time to play the violin. That's what brings me a lot of joy. So whatever job I choose, there must be room for the little things that fulfill me also in a personal way. On a professional level, I know that I want to learn and develop myself, I want to keep my intellect challenged and grow into a great leader.

You grew up in a multicultural environment. In which way did this experience shape your lifestyle choices?

I feel grateful for having a home in both the Indian and German traditions. Both of them have so many beautiful aspects. Germany has been a wonderful place for me to grow up and the social stability is something I don't take for granted. The fact that we are safe when walking down the streets, that we don't need to live in fear, that we have access to free education and a great health system is such a privilege! I am also thankful for the people in my life here in Germany, and I learned from an early age that Germans and Indians are very different, but I find beauty in the different perspectives and lifestyles. In Germany, people are very open and direct in their communication, and they do cherish privacy a lot. In India, people put more emphasis on the family and on sharing time with each other. Also eating is a really big thing! And: You're never alone in India. Somebody will always come speak to you – might it be at home or in the train. In addition to this, spirituality is highly important for many people in India. Sometimes, I find myself in this border zone in between both cultures, and it's not always comfortable to be there. For example, at the family table in an Indian family, there is something like a respect for hierarchy. And when your elder family members have a certain view about any topic, it's very uncommon for you, in particular as a young woman, to oppose that view. I grew up in Germany where we just say what we think. I have observed my mother feeling ashamed of me when I do that and of course, I do not want to hurt my mother's feelings. As a child, this often made me feel lost in translation. But with friction, you grow, and this again is a beautiful experience that has helped me to find out who I truly am – a colourful mosaic containing many pieces of both cultures.

How do you decide when to be German and when to be Indian?

I try to find a balance with my inner value system. So, for example, tolerating or accepting a view that I really find wrong or injust is like betraying my inner self. There have been many occasions in which I did not speak up as a young person because I did not want to be disrespectful to my family. But afterwards, I regretted it and it left a bitter aftertaste. Reflecting about it later on, I came to the conclusion that I find it important to be a role model for other young Indian women, to show them that we also have a voice and there is a space for us – within the family in the society – to share our views. Some of my relatives have even told me to watch my words and not to give a bad example to young women! But sometimes, you just need to listen to your heart. It's also what I mean with overcoming the crisis of character. It's not always easy to stand up for your values, but it's what prevents you from losing orientation in life!

In which way do you bring your multiculturality into the workplace?

Having grown up in a multicultural world, I have become more sensitive towards other people's needs, in particular towards people with a different background. I have always worked in international teams and it's very important to me that nobody feels left behind. So, I make sure, if somebody in the team is not doing well, to understand what we can do to make them feel more at ease. Sometimes it's about listening to others, and sometimes it's about sharing knowledge about hidden rituals or procedures that may be obvious in one culture but may be completely alien to a person who was brought up in a different culture. For example, in Germany, it's not too common to speak about your family at the workplace. I have had colleagues from Brazil or Arabic-speaking countries that felt not cared for because nobody ever asked them how their families were doing! So interculturally-informed communication is important when you work with people from different cultures and want to have good team dynamics.

What do you find fascinating about polymer chemistry?

For me it is absolutely fascinating to understand what holds the core of the world together, just as Johann Wolfgang von Goethe wrote it in his masterpiece Faust. To dig deeper and deeper and to finally understand nature or systems on their molecular level. It gives me so much satisfaction and peace, to understand the root of why things are the way they are. For example, why is the sky blue or how is the evolution of mankind encoded in our DNA. Well, it is all based on molecules! So for me chemistry is my path to unravel the world and it has made me a curious and humble person at the same time.

Right now, I'm finishing my PhD in polymer chemistry and our vision is the 3D printing of organs. When, for instance, a patient needs a new liver, the vision is, that one can create a liver for them from their own cells instead of transplanting one. My little contribution toward making this a reality is to research materials that could be useful for the development of such artificial organs. In science, we are currently at a stage where this concept already works for less complex tissue, such as cartilage or spinal discs. But for more complex organs, like liver, heart, or the brain, further research is still needed. A big challenge is, in a living organism, cells communicate with each other in many different ways and through so many different layers of tissue. When you cultivate artificial tissue, you need to make sure that you keep the communication flowing, otherwise there is no chance of proper organ development.

I actually never thought that I'd end up studying polymer chemistry. My original plan was to study business management because I grew up with a family business and I had a strong interest in leadership topics. But after school, one day before the application deadline to universities, I realized that I had learned all my chemistry textbooks by heart and felt suddenly very sad that my chemistry horizon would stay so limited. The same day I discovered a program that combined business management and chemistry at the University of Ulm in Germany. It seemed to be the perfect match! After several months in this course, I found out that chemistry is such an intense and complex field, that you need to dedicate yourself one hundred percent to it. So in the end, I decided to be courageous and go all in — I signed up to study chemistry.

What were your key learnings from working in research?

When you work in research, I think you need to learn how to bring up a lot of tolerance for frustration. This might sound discouraging, but it is actually a very humbling experience. You learn how to fail and stand up again.

Because everything is so complex and new, you cannot spend a day without failing at least once. And then you keep going and you courageously search for the tiny detail that made you fail. And sometimes this costs you a lot of time and requires an amount of patience I didn't think I would be able to give. There was one period in my PhD where it took me one year and four months to understand one little molecule to the level of detail that was needed in order to finally have a break through. When I started the project, I thought it would take me three months, but then there were many more challenges that I hadn't anticipated. So I followed through and finally got to the piece of knowledge that I needed to solve my problem. Keeping my curiosity alive and being persistent is something I learned in my PhD and which has now become a part of my skillset.

You studied at Stanford. What are the differences between the US and Germany from a researcher's point of view?

Let me just state clearly that what I share is very subjective. What I really loved about Stanford was the inspiring spirit of the people that come together in this incredible place of science and innovation. The people there are so ambitious, passionate, and striving for a better world. My professor was so intrinsically motivated to understand his field of research that his eyes did shine brightly when I showed him some new data. The way research is done over there is very focused on collaboration and it seems that you have more freedom to explore. The feedback style is very constructive, and researchers are encouraged to find their own little area of passion. While this experience may have been very much linked to the professor I worked with, structurally, I think there is a difference in culture at the workplace. Researchers really find a big passion for what they do. Everybody has a big vision. It's maybe a little bit romantic to believe that everybody can change the world just by having a big vision, but I do think it helps to keep doing your best, every day, even when you are not discovering anything new. It's what keeps you going through periods of frustration. Being driven by a vision that is bigger than yourself, also allowing emotions to occur, even in science. Germans try to focus more on the facts rather than on communicating the vision and a storyline to connect the single dots.

Having experienced this has had a deep impact on me, particularly when it comes to leadership. When you lead a team, I find it really important that the team knows your vision and that the team shares this vision. If you don't have a compelling vision, how would you ever attract the brightest minds?

What else do you want to share with the readers?

Wherever I look, I see so much unused potential in our world. If every person had the chance to dedicate their full potential to the world, I think we would be a much happier global community. So many young people around the world want to contribute to the world, and somehow, we make it very difficult for each other to do so. I always wonder how we can not only encourage people to make the best use of their potential, but to also create the structures in which these potentials can be appreciated adequately.

In my view, our society urgently needs to redefine the term "success." We need a shift from a "success for ego"-perspective to a "success for society"-view. This will automatically influence the way we as a society make our decisions. To tackle our ecological and social crisis, it is crucial that we ask ourselves: What value did I create for society? Or: What did I contribute to the larger goal? Answering the last two questions in a profound and honest way and simultaneously being in balance with yourself – that's real success to me. If everybody collaborated to make the best use of their potential, we could together create a very beautiful place. A place where there is gratefulness, appreciation, and a sense of fulfilment. A place where people allow themselves to follow their passions and contribute their talents to something bigger than themselves. A place where we can find bridges between each other and have more empathy for the world we live in. I deeply believe that we have the capacity to build this kind of world. Just imagine what this world would be like if every human being felt a sense of belonging and if every single human being knew that their actions and choices truly mattered!

Beautiful brains change tomorrow...today
Brain-brush reflection exercise:

How did I feel when I read this?

What did I learn?

What will I integrate into my daily life?

Every minute on Twitter should be a minute well spent

Dr. Tu-Lam Pham,
founder of DigitalIQ

What are you most passionate about?

I have always been very passionate about learning and education. I come from a Vietnamese family, where parents tend to take education very seriously. They expect their children to do well in school. It's something like a running gag, that there are only three career options for Vietnamese children: the medical doctor, the engineer, or the disgrace to the family. But my parents were not really tiger parents. When I was younger, I focused a lot on a fairly traditional career. I did very well in school, and I did a master's degree and a PhD at a reputable university. After some time, I figured that he classic career path was not really interesting. What looks good on paper is not necessarily the thing where you can learn the most. So I started to look into different opportunities and changed my career a few times. I'm currently thirty-six years old, and I think I have changed my career every two to three years in the past decade. It was quite a steep learning experience, because every time I changed career, I had to reinvent myself and master a new skill.

When we think about education, it's quite common that we associate it with very formal academic education, but not so much education in life skills. We don't really learn how to reflect on our goals. I'm a big fan of self help books, even when they may have a cheesy reputation. Yes, in the end, it often boils down to a very simple message such as "follow your passion," but I think the important thing is the structured process of reflection that these books can teach you. Many young people spend maybe just one percent of their time on personal reflection and ninety-nine percent on formal education. How about a fifty/fifty split? Another source of excellent free education are YouTube videos and podcasts. There is so much amazing content available online. Today, we can have an education that is better than any master's or PhD for free!

What are the challenges of digital education?

The challenge I see is that it's very difficult to figure out the difference between good and bad content. If you don't really know how to navigate the online world, you might end up just wasting your time playing video games or watching cat videos. It seems to be that the level of education of the parents often determines how they deal with this, how to navigate through this digital world in a healthy way. It means that better educated families are in a better situation to teach their kids how to manage risks of addiction and how to find the most relevant content for healthy and beneficial consumption of digital opportunities. In Germany, we are lagging behind, so I hope to help our citizens get back on track by providing good content. When it comes to access to broadband internet, or artificial intelligence, or even our education systems, we have so much room to improve. For the maybe five percent of our population who are really well educated, digitization can bring plenty of benefits. It can make you extremely efficient, almost superhuman in the way that a single person can create an app or a video that reaches millions of people all over the world. Unfortunately, our education system doesn't really show us how to make the best use of these opportunities and they are unused by the majority of the population. The question is: What do the other ninety-five percent of the population do? How can we as a society help them access this? It's one of the biggest challenges that our society is facing today. My purpose is to contribute to providing affordable access to education, in particular in the area of digital transformation.

Everything changes: the way we work, live, learn. Our entire economic system changes, and it changes really fast. Look at the iPhone. It's only ten years old. Look how it has changed the way we live our lives. I'm afraid we cannot really rely on governments to solve this problem for us! There won't be any party that will come to power and revolutionize the entire existing system, at least not in Germany. So I think, the responsibility is with each of us. And those who don't have the knowledge should at least be aware that it is important to seek out and be open to learning. This could be as simple as the basics of coding or just learning about the opportunities that new digital models can bring to us.

How can you smooth this transition so that it is not based on fear and anxiety?

Even in our digital world, it's very difficult to hire good people, especially to small and medium-sized companies. So they have to train their employees in the most effective way, and also they need to understand that they will be the ones who benefit the most. This means that companies should bear the costs of training, or at least subsidize these costs. Not only in terms of money, but also in terms of time. I think it's also very important to create this space for employees to actually learn a skill they want to learn. So maybe introduce something like Friday as a skill or training day, where people learn new things, and learn to apply these new learnings immediately. Companies could also use this time to ask their employees to develop proposals for what they think the organization needs to learn. Google had this famous twenty percent rule, where employees could spend twenty percent of their time to work on whatever they wanted to work on. This works well in settings where you have intrinsically motivated employees. I think there is some kind of middle way. Unfortunately, there are so many people out there that are so self-satisfied with the status quo and who don't have an intrinsic motivation to change, to become better versions of themselves. You shouldn't just run around and scare people about the future, and still, I think it is important that we make very clear to people how fast the world is changing and how profound these changes are. At the same time, we need to lay out the exciting opportunities that come with these changes. There is so much to gain by adopting innovation! Now you have college dropouts who just build amazing companies. Digital transformation reduces the barriers to entry. It takes away the power from formal gatekeepers and gives power to the crowd. You don't have to audition with people to give you a job anymore. If you know how to code, you can just build an app. If you learn how to create great online content, you can become successful with very few resources. All you need is your idea, a little bit of passion for it, and then just go and test it.

How do we keep up with digital change?

One book that I really like is *Drive* by Daniel Pink. It's about how we can discern intrinsic and extrinsic motivation, with the latter being money, titles, and reputation. There are three pillars of intrinsic motivation: autonomy, mastery, and purpose. Autonomy means that you don't have anybody who will tell you what to do or how and when to do it. Mastery is about craftsmanship, it's about enjoying the process of learning what you are learning. Purpose is about doing something that you find useful. It doesn't necessarily have to be to save the world, it can just be that you want to contribute to your family or to your community. You can just do a quick check on yourself: Out of these three pillars, how many check marks can you make? When I apply this framework to my own life, I can clearly see that autonomy has always been quite important to me. After my PhD, I founded an e-commerce company, then worked in media and venture capital. I always valued autonomy and independence, which can be found the most when you work for yourself. Also, I only want to work on things that are interesting to me. Right now, I teach the principles of digital business, e-commerce, and social media to different audiences. I have been doing this for years, yet I'm still in the process of achieving mastery. I'm trying to become a master by delivering keynote speeches, trainings, and even as a consultant. I need to stay knowledgeable about the latest trends, so I learn something new every day. I also create YouTube videos, or podcasts, and I blog on LinkedIn. With each additional speech, I become a better speaker. My intrinsic motivation is to tell a more interesting story, rather than just repeat the same content every single time. Sometimes I feel a bit stupid: I'm this old guy trying to learn things such as editing a video, that in today's world every twelve-year-old does on the fly. It can feel like a waste of time, but it's all part of the process of acquiring new skills.

For some types of skills, in-person seminars or coachings might be helpful. Self-discipline is very important in a context where you are flooded with information. Many people have already bought many books and bought many online courses, that they never finish. So stick to one and get it done, that's important. There's this book called *The Compound Effect* by Darren Hardy, and its main idea is that small actions add up over time. So if you eat a candy bar today, you will not get fat tomorrow, and if you don't eat it today, you will not get slim either. But if you ate a candy bar every day for the next ten years, it might make you at least twenty kilograms heavier; not eating any candy bar might make you a lot healthier. Habit building is about understanding that there are no quick fixes for long-lasting behavioral change but that it's about a commitment to work on it every single day.

Finding good teachers is another part of the equation. Can you find a trainer who helps your employees stay motivated along the process? Ultimately, what needs to change for a more sustainable future of education is the appreciation and perception of teachers. In Germany, it seems to me that teachers are not really held in high regard; they are not really well paid, their work is not appreciated in an economic sense. Some people even think that if you're a teacher, you were not good enough to do some real job, such as, if you're a math teacher, that you were not good enough to work as a mathematician somewhere. In Asia, for example, teachers have a completely different reputation. This attracts more talent into the teaching profession. This in turn also increases the respect that pupils have of their teachers, and the acceptance of their teachings.

How do we find relevant digital content?

First, we need to find our trusted sources. It could be a media publication, such as the *New York Times*, which, for example, might be more trustworthy than *Breitbart News*. What is actually a lot more relevant in today's fast changing world, though, is to identify experts and influencers in the media world. Many of the very smart people or journalists today do not really work for newspapers anymore, they work independently. They have become bloggers, or podcasters. This is where the most up-to-date sources of information come from. Some bloggers have been blogging about the same industry or area for ten years or so. It's all they talk about; whether they write about economics or politics, whether they review cameras or MacBooks, you know that due to their exposure over a longer period of time, they know what they are talking about. They're probably one of the five or ten most knowledgeable people in the world for their micro topic. If you want to gain deep technical expertise about self-driving cars, it's probably better to follow people who spend sixty hours a week doing nothing but reading about self-driving cars than hearing from someone who only spends an hour a week or so on that topic. If you have access to these experts, you will get the best information.

So the secret sauce to thriving in this digital world is to learn how to master curation of information. Imagine you have a trusted friend who you think is very knowledgeable about health or fitness. If they recommend five sources to you, you can trust that these sources are more valuable than just randomly searching on the internet. So it's just an intuitive approach to learning. Find the human curators online whom you can trust. Trust is very personal, but what I find good indicators for trustworthiness are values and your experience of this person based on your observing them. Being a good curator means that you don't need to tell your friends what they should do or not do, but increase their awareness about where you find good sources of information and what views you have. Why should everyone replicate each other's work? It would be a waste of human resources. We should know whom to ask when we want to know about a topic. But we don't need to all be experts in the same field! And when we are good curators and know how to find other curators, we don't need to go to university anymore. We can just learn everything online. We learn it through our friends and in a way that we find most helpful and fun. It's just so much more effective. We just have to be wise in choosing whom to trust so we don't unnecessarily expose ourselves to fake news. But even with renowned media, there is this risk that, due to cost pressure, they didn't do thorough fact checking either. High quality investigative journalism costs a lot of money, and many newspapers do not have access to these resources anymore. So many of them will just copy and paste what they have found online and turn it into an article. So there is no black and white.

What I personally do is: If I want to know more about a topic, such as, self-driving cars, then I start off with finding one expert in that field. If I don't know any expert yet, because I'm a rookie to the field, I'll be a bit creative and think about companies that are famous for that. And most likely I'd come across Elon Musk as an easy starting point. I'll follow him on Twitter and look at who he follows, and if the big CEO of Tesla follows fifty people who talk about self-driving cars, this can give me a good indication that these guys are very likely to be experts in this field. I can consume the publications, videos, or podcasts they release or recommend. This is a very simple and intuitive way of developing an understanding of the trustworthy influencers in a field of my interest. It's not too different with friends, right? You have maybe one really good friend and then the friends of this friend are quite a good fit to your personal taste. And over a short period of time, I can become my own expert, by reading different perspectives, listening to different podcasts, and subscribing to different YouTube channels. I don't consume too much of one channel or one person, just to keep a good diverse portfolio of information sources. Knowing how to build up your information pool is quite a powerful tool.

And how do you personally evaluate the quality of the content that you see?

First of all, there is something like a subjective measure. You know easily, if you like something or not. I like people who are funny and intelligent, so not necessarily the people who have the loudest voices, the most popular ones, but maybe the ones who have an original perspective or display a point of view that not everybody easily agrees to. Sometimes it's quite interesting to read some more contrarian points of view. Even if you don't agree with them, you get a very different perspective and this kind of helps you to shape your own understanding of the world.

It's also helpful to ask yourself: In which way did I benefit from this piece of content? Sometimes the answer is not at all, and then you just try to consume less of this content. This is a reason why many people have stopped consuming the news, because they say, hey, learning about the newest stupid actions from Donald Trump doesn't really help me grow in any way. Consuming things that don't help them grow or that don't put them into a situation where they can change anything, or make them upset, are not very helpful at all. So they put themselves under a self-imposed media diet.

There are also some more neutral indicators you can look at. If you see that an article has many likes, shares, and positive comments, there is a higher likelihood that this may be an article worth reading. You can scroll the comments before you dive into the article. You can also see which of your friends has interacted with this article in which way. Let's say I follow fifty experts on Twitter and five of those share this one article. If I am really interested in that field, it's probably at least worth a look. So recommendations from people I identify as experts can be a good lead. The problem is that you end up in a filter bubble, if you only listen to opinions that you have chosen to listen to. When we choose our circle of influencers, we need to bring in some sense of diversity, so that we don't end up only listening to the Steve Bannons of the world. For newspapers, for example, I try to follow both the liberal and the conservative newspapers.

How do we protect ourselves from information overload?

We all know that we consume too much digital content. We need to build something I call media competence. Not in the sense that we need to know how to use Twitter, but more like how to use it less. This requires us to understand how to make best use of it, make every minute we spend on Twitter a relevant one. I like to compare digital content to sugar: It's very addictive, and it's very harmful if you consume too much of it. Producers of digital content, very similar to producers of sugar, know very well how to make people addicted. It's what they optimize for because this is how they generate revenues. The problem is that very few consumers actually know how to get themselves out of this situation. This includes myself too. So I think digital detox is very important. I'm not super disciplined, but I try to set up days where I barely consume any internet or set up website content blockers when I work. This helps to protect me from reading certain blogs or websites for a specified period of time. And the only thing I can then do is the task at hand on my computer. You could also just program your Wi-Fi router to shut off after a certain time at night or move your phone out of the bedroom.

I think it's our job as parents to teach our children how they can protect themselves from becoming addicted to digital content. And we have to be role models in that. The interesting thing is that in Silicon Valley, many employees who work at companies such as Facebook or Google, don't allow their kids to use digital services. At Apple, you see more and more parents who do not allow their kids to have an iPhone before the age of sixteen because they know how addictive it becomes.

What would you teach your children?

I would teach my children to be very independent and autonomous. I'd love to build our own school curriculum in a way that we teach them a way of self-reliant thinking. In this way, they can see where they stand for themselves and do not become dependent on their teachers or their parents to tell them what they should learn and in which way they should learn it. Today, being a professional video game player is a very big thing. And just ten years ago it was considered totally stupid. So who knows what it is that is important for my kids to learn? Maybe they come home one day and tell me what it is they want to study and that day I don't grasp it. So I won't be able to help them with their decision! I'd need them to understand for themselves what is a relevant skill they want and need to learn. For this, self-confidence and a skill to reflect on yourself and your role in the world are very important things.

We often do stupid things in our lives because of insecurity, because we are not happy with who we are. This may make us go out and hurt other people so that we feel better. We become victims of peer group pressure, and we let this happen so many times because we don't have the confidence to speak up. How can you speak up if you don't know what to speak up for? You'd need to know your values to do so. Self-reflection is the foundation of everything. And emotional stability should be at the core of it. Academic skills are just built on these foundations. They are useful skills, but they are not very solid. Building a strong solid foundation for life is where people should spend most of their time. There are many ways to build this. I wouldn't claim that I know all the answers. I'm just staying curious and trying to learn more about myself and see what I can pass on to my kids. But one thing I think they should learn is: the patience to wait for things to happen. Not hunting for instant gratification. Being able to make short-term sacrifices or investments that will pay off in the long term.

What other insights do you want to share with us?

Every minute there are so many new and different things that come into our world, and maybe the first step for each of us is to just get rid of complexity first, to be able to see clearly. We then see what is left, and we may get bored because there is nothing left to do. That is the moment when we can come up with new creative ideas about what to do with our lives.

I really like everything that has to do with minimalism. A minimalist is not necessarily a person who lives in a wooden hut that has nothing inside, who has isolated himself or withdrawn from society. Minimalists try to get rid of all the superfluous things that we don't really need in our lives, so they can focus on the things that actually matter to them. It's about creating space to enjoy what we really want to enjoy. So for some, this may be having four pairs of shoes rather than owning one hundred pairs. In an extreme case, you could consider getting rid of people in your life, maybe people who are a bad influence for you or maybe people who are just always asking you for favors but who never really contribute anything to your life. Or maybe those people are not even negative but you just spend so much time maintaining the relationships, like going to events to meet them when you don't necessarily enjoy it.

I'm not really spiritual, but I think, sometimes, when you want to listen to your inner voice, it helps not to have too many outside voices speaking to you. So it can help to get rid of friends, families', colleagues' voices, and get rid of all the media noise for a moment, going into meditation or into digital detox. There's this Japanese woman, Marie Kondo, who is currently trending in the minimalism mainstream. She is on TV making people get rid of their belongings. She will ask you to look at your belongings, something like a T-shirt, and ask one thing: does this spark joy in you, when you look at it? It's not about whether it was expensive, whether you will wear it again next year, or whether it's still there because someone gave it to you. You can only keep it if it genuinely sparks joy in you. Her show is not really just about throwing things away. It's about making space for positive things to appear. Maybe minimalism is at the core of thriving in a fast-changing digital age. I guess this is a good rule for everything in my life. Do I enjoy hanging out with the people that I meet? Do I enjoy the things that I own? And if I can say without a doubt, yes, then I know I'd need to focus even more on them, and the other things, I'd need to leave aside. This is in particular true for the ones that create anxiety in my life! Make sure you have a few commitments that you really care about, and get rid of the irrelevant ones.

Beautiful brains change tomorrow...today
Brain-brush reflection exercise:

How did I feel when I read this?

What did I learn?

What will I integrate into my daily life?

Part Two:

How to Become Good Contributors

Courage and curiosity: leadership in the Digital Age must drive a cultural revolution

Dr. Hans Werner Hagemann,
founder of Munich Leadership Group and co-author of the book The Leading Brain: Powerful Science-based Strategies for Achieving Peak Performance

What is the problem that you're currently solving?

There are many problems to solve, however, there is one question that I'm currently deeply engaged in: How can companies master digital transformation? How can they prepare their executives to be the leaders for this transformation in the VUCA world? From a brain perspective, the new challenges are increased speed and systemic insecurity. To cope with these challenges, we need a new leadership behavior: A leadership behavior that is different from what most leaders are currently ready to offer. And if you look beneath the surface, the underlying question is: What's the purpose of what we're doing here? We are currently undergoing a revolution in business life that is in its impact comparable to the industrial revolution. And so far, only a few companies have understood that it is mainly a *cultural* revolution, driven by the digitization.

In our executive development work, the most typical setup of a company used to be one where there was a leader, and then employees that reported into the leader. There used to be a clear line of reporting and a clear hierarchy, and employees and leaders knew who was responsible for whom and what. There was a dedicated human space for building trust in these relationships: it was built over time. Teams and their members had clearly defined tasks over a longer period of time, and team members could rely on a certain degree of stability in the external environment. Leaders had a clear idea of how their work would create impact, and they had a clear view of how their work would affect the whole environment in which they operated.

What has changed significantly, is that most work in companies is not executed as the typical line work any longer, but it's project work. And even more — not just project work — also work in a matrix on the inside with "dotted lines" to others. These can be players from different eco systems, such as freelancers, millennial start-up personalities, or competitor institutions.

You don't work in your stable team environment anymore, but you work in many different project relationships. It takes some time to understand how team members react to different situations. This creates stress, and this stress is replicated as new projects start. Stability that we found in the former way of collaborating is being replaced with insecurity. Here is the catch: Our brains are not prepared to work like this. We are wired for certainty: we like security and sustainability.

When this level of basic certainty breaks away, we easily get stuck in states where we have no immediate practical solution, and we feel stressed and uncomfortable. Change is not good or bad by definition; however, it has an effect. Insecurity leads to a situation where people are very careful with their decision-making and actions, especially when the environment acts in the same way. It's a little bit like a snowball effect: the more insecurity, the more unstable the whole situation gets.

Currently many leaders are waiting for the situation around them to develop, and they don't take action which is exactly the opposite of how they need to act in the world described above. They need to make decisions all the time, at a fast pace, even in little iterative steps. But instead, many have learned that tomorrow the problem might have changed: If they put efforts into creating a fast, new solution, overnight this solution might have already turned obsolete because the underlying problem has already changed. They try to keep as many options open as possible, which, again, fosters insecurity. This learned passivity-by-fear is a massive threat to transformation. Due to the fear, our brains are put into a situation where they cannot be open-minded and create new solutions. Our brains rather go into a freeze mode: Let's not create more instability in the system, let's wait and hope for something to happen. Let's wait for the situation to change. This is comparable to the reaction of the rabbit in front of the snake: it is "frozen" and finally gets eaten. Passivity kills innovation.

An entire organization can be paralyzed because everybody in the organization is waiting for a clear pattern of data which provides orientation to make decisions. Especially in hierarchical organizations, the leaders are looking at the top management. The problem is: nobody can reliably foresee the big developments. And on the other hand, simply waiting is not a good option at all.

We work with many companies on digital transformation processes. To be really successful, we focus on the *cultural* transformation. It's the question of how to help people become more open to change, rather than experiencing it as a threat. The more fear leaders feel, the more they fall back into old, well-established patterns of behavior that have proven to be helpful in the past. The thing is: the current situation is not comparable to the past, and the well-proven solutions from yesterday don't work anymore.

How can we overcome this decision paralysis?

I think courage is the key word for success. We need people that will take a stand. We need people who will say they believe in a certain future and they will invest in their idea. We help create ecosystems that allow leaders to be courageous. In a corporate setting, it can be very dangerous for your career to take a stand. If you advocate for the wrong option, you might be out tomorrow. Let's take Brexit as an example. Politicians' discussions about Brexit has implications for many businesses. Just imagine you were BMW. When somebody asked you if you'd still build the 'Mini' in England after Brexit, what would you answer? Your answer would probably be very political because you honestly can't really decide what is a good decision when you feel that you need more information. Now this will have a ripple down effect in the organization because this will have an influence on purchasing and recruiting decisions and so on.

Courage means making decisions, and decisions channel the energy in a company. Decisions make companies strong and aligned at the right point in time. Don't be too afraid of wrong decisions. We found out that wrong decisions are less expensive than those decisions that had been postponed — if you have developed your company or team appropriately. Courage only develops in environments that allow mistakes and learn to pivot quickly if necessary. This is the main focus of our work: establish a culture of speed and agility that utilizes mistakes and creates courage.

How do you help clients in need of a transformation process?

We work with our concept of curiosity-based transformation. Human brains need dopamine if we want to really create new solutions and foster innovation. We have experienced that the conventional attempts to change a company culture do not work for a reason. Posters and screensavers bring up the "New 5 Corporate Values" created by an advertising agency with all those bells and whistles. Town halls are impressive and promise a new and better world. But after the spectacular two-day show with all board members and the great party in the evening, during the next work meeting with his or her team, the superior behaves in the same old way and discloses the initiative as lip service. Moreover, the team members are left disappointed and have learned once more: our company will always stay the same.

We design *curiosity-based transformations* where change really happens. We create curiosity, we create new behavior, *leaders do not announce but they act*; and then the brains of all involved are eager to learn. Everyone must be on their toes during the transformation process. It is the demonstrated behavior that counts, not the words. And in hierarchical organizations, as nearly all of the companies are — even if they pretend not to be — each change comes from the top.

Behavioral change is the hottest thing in executive development, and it is at the top and the bottom of each cultural change. Knowing about the brain is key. We believe that there are four main factors that support a cultural shift from fear of change to seeing the opportunities that arise from transformation.

First, it's the clarity over the target state of a company. How attractive is this target state to different groups within your organization? How much growth is there between now and then, and how do you define growth? Your brain produces a lot of dopamine, when you find a target attractive and you work towards achieving this target, and you will be very enthusiastic about working towards this bigger goal. Let's take for example revenue growth. If you wanted to double revenue in the next two years, to whom would this be attractive? As the CEO — it might be attractive for you because you may end up on the cover of Time Magazine as Manager of the Year, but what is the benefit for other people in your company? The people may be very scared of revenue growth pressure because they might not know how to fulfill those expectations. The Chief Operating Officer might think we don't have the tools, we don't have the factories, we don't have the materials to produce these many goods. If people start to doubt that your target is good for them, it will be a threat to them and their environment. What we need to do, is to translate the benefits of the target state into what is attractive to the groups or even individuals involved. Change a is a very subjective matter!

The second factor is the consequences of doing nothing. We call it "intelligent pain pressure". This intelligent pain pressure is necessary in addition to the target attractiveness. For example, if you want to stop smoking, you could say: hey, every time I don't smoke, I save money, and I will put this money in a piggy bank and after a while, I can go on a wonderful vacation. This could be an attractive target. But still — why should you stop smoking? There are many ways to create intelligent pain pressure. It can be very different for different people. Most people are sensitive to a social push, they can utilize the support from their social environment for creating it. Not wanting to fail a public commitment can be a good nudge to not smoke again.

You can also imagine this on an organizational level. Companies can play with different incentives helping their employees not engage in behavior that by all means is considered harmful. From a neuroscientific point of view, this happens through group norm behaviors. We know our brain feels significant pain when we find ourselves in situations that indicates us, we are socially excluded. Being socially excluded is a big punishment to us humans, since we are a social species. We naturally form our "tribes," even in the workplace, and we naturally try to belong to these "tribes." When you agree on certain group norms, you have an intrinsic motivation not to engage in behavior that will result in you being excluded from the "tribe." Another example is creating inner circles of opinion leaders within a company. Naturally, people don't want to be kicked out of these circles, once they have attained the status, so they have an incentive to contribute to developing the group.

Intelligent pain pressure is the most influential of the four factors, up to eighty percent of the change effect can be linked back to it. The word "intelligent" is important because it's a skill not to push it too hard, otherwise you end up on the negative side, that is, you create an environment where people act out of fear for being socially excluded. That would be what we call dumb pain pressure. It would lead to a situation where people spend their energy finding ways to stay in the group at any price rather than solving an inconvenient problem in a creative way. When companies start to tell employees that they need to do X, else they will be fired, employees spend most of their energy calling up lawyers and friends to find out if that threat is real or not, rather than focusing on their work. You need to find the sweet spot, where you create a little bit of a challenge, but don't instill fear.

The third factor is the employee's own assessment of their skills and knowledge: Do I have the prerequisites that I will need to be successful in my new role in the future? It's easy to answer, when you have a clear understanding of what is needed. You can offer and participate in qualification trainings to support the changes. It's just that companies easily overlook this when they design their transformation programs. We had a case in a company that had decided to completely transform its business. They went from a regular heating business into fuel cell technology. And one of the company's top performers raised this concern that he might not be the right guy to lead this transformation. He said, "I don't know if I can perform with this new technology. I'm not an expert. I am in doubt." He was still very enthusiastic, and he was a fast learner. The reaction of the colleagues was: "Hey, don't worry about it. You will easily make it happen. If you don't succeed, nobody will." It was a well-meant motivation attempt, but the psychological effect was actually the opposite of calming because they just put more pressure on this person. He felt that he wasn't being taken seriously and didn't feel like he was in a position to meet the expectations. To help ease some pressure in a situation like that, you will need to listen to the people who are bold enough to raise their concerns. You can ask: "What exactly are you thinking about? What are your feelings behind these concerns?" And then you can take action, offer the right qualification measures, and reduce the fear.

The fourth factor is about the ecosystem of the person involved in the change process. The exact question is: Will my personal environment support me in the path to our goals? The personal environment can be the team, the peers in the company, it can be family, it can be friends — anybody who is relevant enough to be in their inner circle. If the company moves in one direction, and everyone in their professional environment supports them, there are still the needs of family to reconcile with. Because if they don't feel happy with the decision, the employee may end up not feeling happy either. For a company, this is important to know. We had a situation with a client where a young, high potential manager was asked to move to Poland to lead a new factory there. It was a great offer, and he had a brilliant future in the company ahead. It was one of the most important strategic positions in the company at that time. He was very hesitant to accept the offer, and we were wondering what was behind this resistance. It turned out that his wife was a great tennis player. She was actually the local tennis champion, and she did not want to leave her local tennis club. It sounds so simple, but during transformation processes, we often overlook these simple but critical facts. We want to change, but we are not the lone decision-maker in our lives.

In a case like this, how do you make sure that companies do not abuse the private information of their employees?

That's a very valid concern. You must respect the employee and his or her family. Ethics is very important here. You can help to create an array of options that are in line with the interest of the family. It turned out that his wife was not hesitant because she didn't like to go to Poland in general, but more that she didn't know about the options of playing tennis there. For the company, it made sense to invite the young couple there and have them explore the opportunities by themselves. What the company can do is to help gather data points for the family to decide. There are fine lines between information transparency, influence, and manipulation, and dealing with these is an important part of the company culture. But it's never wrong to provide more information upon which people can make their own decision. Don't hold back information that you think may harm someone just because you want to protect someone. Doing so, you are starting to manipulate, even if your intentions are good. Think about it: you would put yourself above the other person. Ingeborg Bachmann, a famous German writer and poet, once said: The truth is reasonable to man. There are also plenty of examples in practice where people manipulate others to fulfill their own expectations. Influencing is different from manipulation in an important way. It is very natural; we do that already in the morning, standing in front of our closet and deciding what to wear. Obviously, when we have important meetings, we want to look in a certain way — we want to influence the people we meet, and there is nothing bad about it.

The core value in this case is integrity. The company wanted to provide all the information that it found and not withhold relevant information that might have been supportive of a move to Poland. Holding back relevant information is manipulation. When you want to act out of integrity, you provide all information, and you are open for the other person to make their own decision.

In general, I think there's a strong need to speak about values in society, and in organizations. To be frank, there are so many people who abuse our systems to the disadvantage of other human beings. This is not okay, and in particular in companies, which are social entities, we need strong value systems. People talk about integrity all the time, but when you look around, there is too little of it in the corporate world.

Leaders must speak about integrity more often, and they must demonstrate it. There should be zero tolerance for violating integrity. The violation of integrity today that has no consequences, is the standard of tomorrow. There are decisions that you have to make as a leader, which may be very difficult decisions. As a leader, find out what your personal convictions are, and then make sure you don't run into a situation where you have to act and speak against these convictions. It's actually one of the top reasons why I'm self-employed and why I have founded my own company. The worst thing for me would be to have somebody forcing me to do things that are not in line with my own values and convictions. It's unacceptable for me.

How do you create a clear value system that you can stick to?

Creating a clear value system in your organization requires clear communication. Value systems are very important for companies because they are important for the health of a company. Clear communication means that you also engage visibly in behavior that supports your values.

As a company, every now and then you need to reassess your value system. In particular, when you are unsure about certain behaviors that you observe, be it from leadership or from team members. And sometimes, at the end of your discussions about values, you will have a clearer understanding of how everyone will demonstrate the company values.

In our company, we never changed our values, but our definition of most of the values has evolved over the course of the time. There were several situations where we were forced to think deeply about the meaning of the values in the context of a certain situation, and — in consequence — of accepting or continuing projects or not. Where is the red line that you will not cross, no matter what? How far are you willing to stretch your definition of your values? It is a continuous conversation about what is right and what is wrong.

Many company leaders think it's sufficient to write down the list of ten top values and then hang it on the walls in the company. But what is lacking, is the *visible behavior* that demonstrates how these values are enacted. Behavior is even more important than mindset, in my point of view. How people interact with each other in and outside of the organization is the unwritten, but true value system. *Doing* something is the ultimate truth. And since top executives tend to be the people everyone looks up to in an organization, their behavior, not their talk, is shaping the company value system. If you see it from a transformation point of view: Employees will certainly notice if their leaders engage in new and atypical behaviors. It's these unexpected triggers that create curiosity within team members as to why and where this change comes from. Eventually this curiosity leads to the conscious engagement with the underlying values and derived behaviors which was intended in the first place.

Can you share a case example of an ethically challenging decision you had to make?

We had one very serious situation when I received information which was absolutely confidential but would massively affect the performance of my client and would probably also have legal consequences. I had come to that information confidentially from a friend because he was having private drinks with someone who was both his friend and a high-ranking executive of a company that was in discussion to be taken over by my client in a merger. Late in the evening, after many glasses of beer, his friend was making fun of the merger and told some stories that he would have better not told. And the question then was, of course, how would I deal with this piece of information? Now that I had it. Would I inform my client at all? If I decided to inform them, how would I go about it? Would I be open about the source? Or would I cover the source of information? How much detail would I give?

I normally discuss such a case with one colleague in our company. What would he do if he was in my situation? Should I say anything at all? I was not really involved in the merger, and I did not have any formal obligation to advise my client on this topic. What was my moral obligation? Unfortunately, having heard this information, I could not pretend that I hadn't heard it. I spoke with my colleague, and we analyzed the situation from all angles. In the end, I thought that I had the moral obligation to mention this information but not speak about the source of the information.

When I spoke to my client, I went up to a level of detail that I could justify to myself and made clear that I thought this was a serious thing. I left it up to him how to deal with this information. I hope that was the right decision, but there's no real way to check what is right or wrong. This is where business becomes very personal — and also somehow a bit fuzzy.

What else would you like to share with us?

I'm a bit concerned about the economic system as it stands right now. It makes people act in certain ways, sometimes without any ethical foundation. It's often purely about creating profit, and those who fulfill this expectation are the ones that succeed. It's about creating situations of short-term advantage for a project or for a company or for somebody who is responsible for something clearly defined in the company. And I think this pressure is increasing. People are not discussing the consequences in depth because it is inconvenient and distracting. Look at the big problems we have, such as plastic garbage in our oceans. I believe the reason for these problems are that we, on the individual, small-scale level, try to create advantage for our small situations because we sometimes seem to be prisoners of a system in which making more profit seems to be the only option to survive. In this system, each person is incentivized to deliver results, and these results are linked to numbers, ending up in increasing profit.

It's not very sustainable, if you aggregate this, and unfortunately, I cannot see a groundbreaking solution for this right now. What I think though, is that we need to analyze and understand the systemic connections of our individual decisions better. May it be in our project, in our company, in our community. I think a more sustainable way of living would be to focus more on the way we interact with each other, how we treat each other, on the very individual level. We should not participate in this rat race for creating more and more profits. We need to learn to see the bigger picture. We all have limited time on earth, and we shouldn't waste our time with too much competition creating all the negative side effects. We should create situations where each of us adds to the other person's happiness. We have *social* obligations, not economic ones. What we should do is build companies where we can balance economic thinking with everything else that is really important to our individual lives.

Beautiful brains change tomorrow...today
Brain-brush reflection exercise:

How did I feel when I read this?

What did I learn?

What will I integrate into my daily life?

Establish mindful collaboration through technology

Urs Merkel, founder at MatchManao

What is most fascinating to you currently?

My personal ambition is becoming a master in bringing people to their personal sweet spot, so that every person can enjoy well-being in the workplace and therefore in life. In my company, we focus on the workplace because that is where most people currently spend their waking hours — we are working minds. The mind from my perspective is nothing physical. It contains all the experiences you have collected during your life — from when you grew up as a child to your current everyday life. This collection of experiences is reflected in your character traits, your personality, and it has a big influence on your value system and work style. Your mind is your treasure chest for your perspective on earth and society. It goes way beyond rational thinking. We named our company MatchManao. *Mana'o* is a Hawaiian concept that describes the perfect symbiosis between your mind, your spirituality, your body, and your skill set. When these elements are in perfect balance with each other, and when you can follow your passion, you can actually reach your sweet spot. It is a step by step process, but it's quite achievable.

How do you balance the "Manao" in a professional setting?

Our scope is currently on matching freelancers with companies, many of them are software engineers. Even when you have legally sorted out all trust limitations, such as non-disclosure agreements, there is still an interpersonal level of trust required. In software development, you need a lot of data. There are many different stakeholders involved, who own different parts of the process and of the data required. We have experienced that with matched teams, compared to control groups, information exchange happens much earlier. We believe that due to increased trust through the matching process, people care more about each other and think more as a team, which makes them be more proactive in their mutual interactions. While in traditional projects, freelancers might have to ask many times before they have all the rights, in a matched team, the stakeholders seem to think ahead and provide all the access rights without asking. Matching has two benefits. One, we help the teams get to know each other faster (because they have a better understanding of each other based on their character data). Second, a structured matching leads to a higher potential of problem solving given a certain set of diversity in mindsets. They will understand each others' opinions more easily because we give them the framework to put each others' opinions into the right context. We collect different data, and we match profiles with each other in ways that research from psychology and organizational behavior has shown to be helpful for team performance. Our key learning was: when you provide transparency in a team context, it helps enhance the communication in meetings and overall, it improves collaboration.

What do you optimize for in your matching models?

We have come to the conclusion that this process of bonding and trust building with each other can be radically shortened, when you consider some structural data in the matching process. There are basic descriptive factors, such as the level of introversion of a person or the value system. These are not necessarily topics that companies look into when they staff a team, but they will have an impact on the quality of interaction of the team in the beginning stages. Researchers have not really yet agreed on what the key variables are to optimize for team performance. So for our everyday work, we have looked at a multitude of psychological models and value systems like the Big Five/ OCEAN model, the Gallup strengths model, Belbin role model, or the MSA model and we just combine essential factors of them and see which models perform best under which circumstances and which help us determine interventions for best outcome in performance of a team. We look at character traits, for example introversion versus extroversion or the level of conscientiousness. Understanding character traits and value systems of people helps to improve your interaction with each other. When teams share a common set of values, they are very effective. Data gathering helps to tailor our interactions in a way that helps teams grow together faster, understand their team purpose better, and find better ways of working together. Overall, it helps to reduce the time gap between the first kickoff and a high performing team — you reach higher levels of productivity in a shorter time. In terms of quantifiable measurement, we look at measures such as productivity rates, retention or fluctuation rates of team members or the number of change requests during the period of a certain project. We then compare the results of teams that were matched with our algorithms against a baseline of randomly staffed teams with comparable external project features as a control group. When we look at the differences in these different indicator levels, we can see how effective our matching is. It sounds a little bit odd, but just the mere fact that people know that they are put into a team not by technical requirements but also by something more human, such as their personality, helps them feel more relaxed in a team. Some might claim it to be a placebo effect, but even if so, it's still helpful, isn't it?

What are the potential downsides of matching people based purely on algorithms?

Well, technology is just a tool. It's like dynamite: you can use it to kill people or to dig holes. What we are doing is to use it for the benefit of humankind, for the well-being of people in organizations where we spend most of our time. Yes, we need to be careful in our matching process not to categorize people. I'm not a prophet and cannot design or decide on ethical value systems for all the other people, but what I would wish is that people see the insights created through data analysis as an opportunity to enhance mutual understanding. If you put only introverted people into one team, then there is a chance that they don't start talking to each other at all, and with extroverts only, chances are, that listening to each other will be a challenge. Now this is a bit exaggerated, just to make it very visual. Homogeneous teams do not perform as well as diverse teams, because they are structurally biased in one direction and so once the team gets off track, there is no one to bring them back on track. So if you really want to build high performing teams, you need a good mix of perspectives and skills. To bring together people who have a strong drive for creating vision, you need the creative heads and you need the people who love to get things done. As you can imagine, the more diversity in perspective in a team, the more room for discussion team members will need. So all in all, you need a solid process that helps heterogeneous teams solve conflicts. We help team members understand underlying behaviors. For instance, when a person is highly introverted, they might not enjoy hanging out after work so much or engaging in small talk. In that example, it's helpful for an extroverted person to have this information so that they do not think they do not like each other. It's not that I don't like you, it's more that I need more space for myself. You create a basis of understanding, which is needed to build trust. The way we design our service is that we use many different matching criteria to ensure there is a high level of heterogeneity in the team. So you can match based on more than your personality traits, you can also match based on role allocation or on your values.

How did you find this fascination for team flow optimization?

Steve Jobs said "you can only connect the dots backwards," and when I reflect back, I don't think there was one specific event. As a child, I played soccer in a team that was very multicultural. There were children from Russia, the Philippines, Turkey, and so on. Diversity was our common denominator. My mum taught me that whatever happens, be honest — at your core, be an honest person because this will give you inner peace. She always told me: "When you don't understand things, don't push them away. There is no one person who is better than another person. Look into the differences. Find out, what makes people see things differently. Everyone has the same right to express their own personality." So there is a very personal aspect to why I do what I do today. And throughout my life, I've worked in several teams, and luckily, most of them were diverse, had a high level of mutual trust, and productivity was high. And I thought: What would it be like to have this kind of team flow experience in every team that I work with? What is the difference between these teams? How could we create such teams in a structured way? During my master studies in data science in California, I took a course called organizational behavior that was taught by Professor Christopher Sterling, a very inspiring teacher and scientist. I learned from him that teams can reach their highest productivity when team members' focus on more than just trying to fit in the right technical skill sets. The decisive impulse that started our MatchManao project came from my co-founder Alexandra. In current staffing approaches, in particular in the software space, we try to staff for roles to balance out seniority. The real drivers of team productivity, however, are in the matching of team members' personalities. It's nothing I invented; there is a lot of research about it. Science found that character traits and value systems are drivers of well-being and productivity in teams. From my experience, the real difference in performance between teams is the quality of their communication and listening. Communication works on different levels. You have active communication, such as writing or talking to each other. Then you also have passive communication, such as body language. The teams where communication flows seamlessly and where there is a high overall status of information transparency, are the ones that perform better because people are not afraid to ask clarifying questions or raise issues early in the process when you still have time to change things. This helps align the actions in the team and helps with prioritization. In teams with high transparency, people can also help each other when there is a bottleneck, and this also helps in improving team performance. It's not only about efficiency, it's also about caring. Transparency is important, but so is the awareness that you are part of one team.

How do you train yourself to understand yourself better?

You can start to become more aware of your feelings by asking yourself, from time to time, where a certain feeling such as anger comes from. Each of us experiences these situations. And then we can ask ourselves: What was the trigger that made me react in this way? What did I do so the other person had the understanding that their behavior was the right answer to my behavior? I'm a big fan of the "*radical honesty*" approach by American psychologist Brad Blanton, which means being honest with yourself, what you really want from life, and being honest with each person you are in a relationship with. He stresses that you need to express your needs and desires so that you understand each other as human beings. It sounds so simple, and yet, it's not really easy to apply to daily life. When you really take this into consideration, it also means that you need to learn how to respect different points of view. It changes the approach in which you interact with people. I practice radical honesty in a way that I try to genuinely express to others how I feel about things or how I understand a situation. My intention is to help the other person understand in which way I might differ from them and to show that it's okay that we are different.

Let me share a more concrete example from my private life: I had always had this wish to own a steel drum, and for my birthday, my dad started a little family and friends crowdfunding campaign. They were really successful, and when I found out about it, instead of feeling happy about it, oddly enough,

I felt very stressed. Managing my own company, sports, reading, and so on, was already a lot of workload, and I felt like adding another activity would not help with my well-being. On the other hand, I also knew how much effort and good intention they had put into the project. I wanted to show them my gratitude, and my appreciation, and I wanted to be authentic. I felt a bit stuck and helpless, and a little bit angry about my decision paralysis as well. In the end, I found the courage to speak up, and told them that I had changed my plans and did not want a steel drum anymore because I had no idea how to find the time to learn to play it. To me, speaking out was a big relief. In the first moment, they were a little bit upset with me. In the end though, they showed empathy with my situation. Feelings are nothing which other people can deny. Nobody can say that your feelings are not true. I think the worst feeling really is when you have too many unspoken feelings stored inside yourself because it will affect all other areas of your daily life as well. My experience is that speaking your feelings can solve issues and misunderstandings because you learn how to communicate clearly. So this radical honesty approach creates transparency, and I feel that this helps with better understanding, better communication, and better relationships. We have so much to learn about our own feelings and about other people's feelings. I think what we need as a societal skill is an understanding that different people have different views, so the same situation can lead to different behavior for different people. Just this alone can help us work together in a more effective way.

What would you like to share with the world?

I would like to invite the readers to acknowledge the diversity in each of us. Every person is unique and therefore we are different from one another. Even if we look similar, and behave in similar ways, there is still uniqueness in each of us. This uniqueness needs to be treated respectfully. There is a deeper sense behind different behaviors that sometimes we cannot see at first glance. So before we judge, I think it is important what we try to gently seek understanding and clarity. If we manage to build this mutual respect into our everyday interactions in our personal relationships, into our teams, I think we can create value. We wouldn't need to design tools like Match-Manao is offering, no need for all the math, and the algorithms.

It sounds intuitive, doesn't it? We intuitively know how to treat each other respectfully. And we should also treat ourselves respectfully. This respect should also include the relationship between our mind and our body. If we listen inside ourselves, we can find our own sweet spot in life. The ex Formula 1 champion Nico Rosberg says that a good team only exists when each of the team members can optimize the balance between their bodies and their minds.

In today's attention economy, we spend way too much time being distracted away from our feelings. We spend time on the screen, we spend time getting things done. Don't get me wrong, I love getting things done, but I also need to remind myself to keep enough space for going for a walk and reflecting on my overall well-being. Sometimes, I don't listen very well to what my body wants to tell me. For example, when I am absorbed in coding, I forget about my body, and this accumulates in chronic back pain. My new year resolution is to enhance my awareness about what is happening inside my body. When I feel stuck, I watch a Simon Sinek video or read one of his books. He is one of the most motivational people for me because in my view, he has understood what is needed for good leadership in today's world. In particular, when you are a leader, you need to communicate very clearly, both in written and spoken communication, that every single member of the team is equally important in this project. The message I try to convey is "No one of us is able to get the job done on our own. We need each other as a team. So if one of us has a problem, the entire team has a problem." I have found it helpful to use project management tools like Trello or Slack to create transparency by spreading information to all team members, so they can see that they are not the only person working. It sounds so simple, but in reality, we sometimes forget this. In our team Slack channel, we greet each other every morning so that everyone knows that the other members are present. I feel that we still have a lot to learn in terms of how to balance out our workload, and I don't see enough people engaging in this field. My fear is, if I'm too scared to do this, and nobody else is doing it either… well, with the current developments in our society I think that we will not have a very happy future. It's really important that we find tools that enable organizations and their employees to work in their sweet spots and feel some kind of happiness in the workplace. I'm not kidding when I say that I think happiness is a human right.

Beautiful brains change tomorrow...today
Brain-brush reflection exercise:

How did I feel when I read this?

What did I learn?

What will I integrate into my daily life?

Learning is about translating a new concept into your own language

Nikolas Schriefer, founder at Stagelink

What is currently your number one topic of interest?

I am really interested in personal development through learning. I get a lot of motivation from learning new skills and understanding new concepts. I think I was already weird as a kid. I'm a trained musician, and I started playing piano at the age of five. I would get up early in the morning and practice the piano before going to school, and it was the first thing I did when I came back home. Not because my parents asked me to do that, it was just really important to me. It feels very good, very rewarding to me, to see how I get better at things. I think it's maybe even a little bit of an addiction. When I was in college, I realized how much I love learning. I loved most classes in school, and I loved music, so I went to music college to study jazz composition and piano. Then I went to business school because I wanted to train in other areas. Even nowadays, when I'm at home, I just watch a tutorial, something that teaches me how to do coding or something about blockchain. It feels more rewarding to me than watching Netflix, and sometimes even more important than going out with friends for a drink. I learn many things in parallel. I am learning practical, technical skills, such as machine learning. I read papers about new research that is published, and I try to build these insights into our models that we use in Stagelink. So I try to apply it and test it immediately; it's learning by doing.

I think that if you really want to learn something, talent is important only to a certain extent, but passion and endurance are so much more important. It's a matter of mindset. If you have this mindset of "no task is too big," and you have a good grasp on how you can split up a task into smaller tasks and validate if you're on track, then you can sort out anything. I think having an iterative and agile approach to learning is very helpful, in particular if you want to build a company and have only limited time and money to do so.

What is your preferred method of learning?

I always learn with a goal in mind. Let's take the piano as an example. I choose a song or a piece of music that I like and that I want to practice, that I want to become good at. And to determine what is good, I use my favorite recordings as a benchmark, that is my finish line. I also start with knowing where my starting point is, which means that I do a mental assessment of how far I am away from this benchmark. When it comes to practicing piano, I have found that the best way for me to reach this goal is to start very slowly. So I start playing a piece very slowly, and I use a metronome to pace myself. I gradually increase the speed, until I have figured out the technical part of the piece and don't need to worry about notes and speed anymore. This is when a different phase of the learning journey starts. This is when I go beyond playing the right notes, when I get into the interpretation of the piece.

I'm quite a structured and analytical person, and I analyze musical pieces before I learn them. There are different dimensions to a piece of music. To put it in very simple terms, I'd say there is melody, harmony, and rhythm. Obviously, they are all interdependent, and still you can dissect a piece and analyze these dimensions separately. To most people, melody is probably the most relatable parameter because it's quite salient and easy to remember. A melody is a succession of notes, one note comes after the other, and the notes have a relationship to each other, but they also have their own contribution to the entire song. In other words, the melody has a relationship to itself, and to the entire song. And the melody has a relationship to the harmony too. There is always this pattern of tension and release in music, the concept of dissonance and consonance. In harmony, it's even a little bit more important than in melody. The two have to fit together, and I need to understand my part in this relationship.

There is also a very important emotional element to music. You need to feel a piece of music, in order to really understand it. People have different skills, and I'd say for me, I'm more skilled in understanding harmony. This is maybe due to my training as a jazz pianist, where harmony is important. So when I learn a new piece, I first analyze its harmony structure. It may not be spelled out explicitly, but it's always implicitly there. For me, the second part of learning starts when I don't have the feeling that I need to control every single note anymore because I know the basics. This requires me to have established a certain routine, a process, like memorizing the notes so I don't need to think anymore. Then I translate it into a language that is a bit closer to my understanding of music — which is harmonic understanding — than what is written on the sheet. This might lead to me not always playing the exact composed notes. Especially when I play it for the first time, I'd actually not even be able to sight read a lot of pieces because I'm just not that well practiced in that. But the important thing is, that I can still play it. Most untrained listeners wouldn't even notice that I don't play exactly what I'm supposed to play, because I improvise, but it still makes sense because it is consistent with the basic structure of the piece.

How do you translate your musical experience into the work you're doing?

Our company Stagelink provides digital marketing software for event promoters in the entertainment market, such as for concerts or shows. What we do is help them find attendees for their events using digital marketing tools. With digitization, we have plenty of opportunities to reach people we could not reach before, people that might be very interested in the event but just didn't know about it. We use online data to create clusters of internet users and figure out what these user groups might be interested in learning about, in attending. And we help the event promoters reach these very specific target groups by displaying relevant ads to them.

Somebody said once: "It's a pity that the great minds of this world are all thinking about how to make more people click more ads." I think this is a very negative way of seeing it, and the statement is not necessarily true. Advertisements are not bad in their nature. Spam is bad. Spam is like cluttering your Facebook newsfeed with announcements that you are not interested in. It's just annoying, isn't it? If my favorite band is coming to town, wouldn't I want to know it? And maybe I'd also be interested in seeing bands that are similar to them. For us, it's about creating awareness about potentially exciting and joyful experiences for people. Our purpose is to help people enjoy great life experiences.

What is your purpose in life?

That's a very philosophical question. It depends on the abstraction level. There can be so many different answers to this, even when I just look at my own life. So for example, at the highest level of abstraction, I actually think that purpose doesn't matter at all. What happens here and now is probably super irrelevant. That's a very depressing view because it also means that nothing in life matters. But at another level of abstraction, there is a state where even the little things matter a lot to me, where I think that it matters whether I enjoy the cocktail I'm drinking or if I close a deal. I want to keep on growing, developing myself. I think this applies not only to me. The feeling of being stuck is quite depressing. And I think it's important, that I am a good leader and create a purposeful work place, a place where well-being matters.

How does that learning apply to your organization?

I think that it is important to get this understanding of how to put yourself into a flow state. I have learned a very helpful technique to get myself into flow for practicing the piano. I play one note, for example the middle C, and I try to really sink into that note, into the sound that it creates. When you have a grand piano, you can clearly hear the overtone series of the note. It's simple physics. The tone is always made up of other sounds, so basically if you play the middle C on the piano, you can hear the C-tone from one octave above. You can also hear other notes such as the G, the E, the B-flat, and so on. The C contains different notes. It's a really cool experience, and it's quite learnable. So when I sink into this tone, I can hear the different other tones that it's made of, and then I can just follow the flow and play some other notes, whatever fits into the flow. It feels a little bit as if the music is telling you what note needs to be played next. So getting into flow is a process. And when it comes to learning in the organization, for me, for example, it requires having a clean and quiet space around me. Even my files are very organized on my computer. If there is clutter around me, it's very difficult for me to get into a productive state of mind. And I have realized this is very different for every person. One part of being a leader is helping others find their best approach to getting into that flow state. This requires me understanding my colleagues' parameters for getting into a flow, the triggers for them to enter and to lose the flow.

I'm very curious, and I like to observe differences in performance in relation to the context. So for example, I'll definitely try to find out what it is that will make you perform well one day and the other day not so much? How come one person is very happy one day and another day not so much? And will happiness lead to higher engagement or higher performance? In our team, we do scheduled feedback talks, and we speak about these topics. I would say something like, "Hey, I noticed that you seemed to have a lot of fun the past few weeks — what was the change that fed into this?" We can learn from each other, and I think ultimately, when each member of the organization is at their best, this is also helpful for the entire organization. And once a month we also do group sessions, where all the different departments come together and share their ups and downs so that they can learn from each other. Software development can learn from the mistakes of the marketing teams and so on.

What have you learned over the past five years of growing the company?

Our company has gone through various stages of development. The first stage was very much about understanding the market and the customer demands, and how we fit in there. It's about finding a solution to a problem that you see. And it needs to solve a problem for a person, for a user. At some point we thought, yes, we have it, and we raised money to grow based on the assumption that our product market fit was right. We built a financial plan that was linked to certain expectations about the number of users, traction, and engagement of the users. And we hired people to reach those projected numbers. But then we didn't reach them, in particular, our revenue projections were too optimistic. So then we entered into a stage of consolidation, and we even had to scale down the business. We had to revisit our target group and pivot our offering. It's a very painful stage in the start-up life because you are at a point where you still have some money in the bank and yet you are spending too much on salaries. The worst thing to do is fire your employees. Letting people go is never easy, and in my view, it shouldn't ever be. We had to let people go because we had to bring the company to sustainable profitability. I didn't want the company to go bust.

My co-founder, Michael, and I were still convinced that the market we were operating in had a big problem and that it needed a solution, and that we had a good chance of contribution to the solution. We brainstormed different ideas across the different departments, selected the three most promising ones, and then we did really fast prototyping for these ideas to see if the market would pick up on them. When you want to test a product for market acceptance, it's important to know the criteria upon which you will decide if the test was successful or not. Otherwise, you will be completely biased. And when you run the test, you need to look at data to see how you perform against the predetermined success criteria. We are a very numbers-driven company. We look into what clients we have, the deal structures, and where and how much we want to grow based on underlying number crunching. So we try to have a very clear view on how to help without draining our resources. Data is also very important to help yourself let go of your psychological bias. Even the most reflected human being might still be subject to some bias. Daniel Kahneman's book *Thinking Fast and Slow* has helped me realize this.

What else would you like to share with the readers?

We spend a lot of time on personal development, and at the same time, we spend a lot of time in recruiting for cultural fit. Having a common ground when it comes to living certain values is important because it affects how we work with each other. We have four core values, that are quite straightforward. One is "navigate adventures." We are looking for people who are bold enough and feel excited about maneuvering through stormy waters. The second is "challenge the status quo." We are a start-up, albeit an established one, and we are challenging the status quo of the way business is done in our industry; it's a little bit like we are trying to go with our heads through walls. It requires confidence. And we often challenge ourselves to see if we are on track. I love to be challenged by my team members. Third is "listen and learn." So yes, please challenge each other, but let's not be arrogant. We can learn a lot from each other, and we can learn a lot from our customers, when we are ready to listen to them. Our final one is "give first." We get a lot of satisfaction from helping others without strings attached. It's also how we run our operations. It requires us to be ready to help without always having the direct reward in mind. When you develop a product that really solves a problem for somebody, then typically you create some value for the other side, and most people are very happy to financially reward you for this. What you do is address a pain and look at that pain from an economics point of view; it's like negative utility. There is a willingness to pay to ease this pain. I don't think too much about pricing and monetization before I think about utility or solving a problem. Obviously, we cannot do everything for free, but many times, we can be a lot more generous than we think.

Beautiful brains change tomorrow...today
Brain-brush reflection exercise:

How did I feel when I read this?

What did I learn?

What will I integrate into my daily life?

Mastery of human relationship building: Every criticism is an opportunity to learn

Jan Dzulko,
founder of Everphone

Let's talk about something that fascinates you.

What matters most to me, are human relationships. My view is deeply rooted in theories from physics, in particular, string theory, that states that everything is a string. I believe that this is what matters most in our universe of humans. For me it's most fascinating to observe and learn from all the different kinds of human relationships. I hope that counts for most people in our world, that humans are more meaningful than objects. And we say that so easily. As if that's clear for everyone, and still, in my everyday life, I observe quite the opposite.

The first time I really got in touch with this fascination was when I reflected upon my marriage. A few years ago, my wife and I started to search for what it means to be a wife or a husband. This deep dialogue between us happened at a point in our relationship where we knew there was something that created tension and frustration in our lives. When I feel attacked, I shut down communication. In that moment, I'm not mindful at all because I become very defensive. In the case of my marriage, it meant that we didn't speak anymore, sometimes for two to three days. Of course, if you live together, at some point in time you need to pick up communication again. When I reflected on my behavioral pattern, it occurred to me that I had lost a few days, highly precious days, in our relationship. We started off very casually, but then our reflections took us into different layers of our relationship. We are friends, we are parents together, we're partners because we own things together, and we're lovers of course. We deconstructed our relationship into its most granular individual parts, and then we started to analyze how happy we were in these different aspects of our marriage. On the surface, it is one human relationship, but we saw very quickly that this one relationship consisted of so many sub-relationships and that these were somehow entangled. I found myself in the middle of a gigantic web of relationships. Not only as a husband, but also as a brother, as a father, as a friend, as an employer, as an investee, as an investor. All these different worlds that exist in our lives, they are based on the nature and the interplay of our webs of relationships.

How can we have reflexive conversations?

We as human beings sometimes find ourselves stuck in social conventions, and when we want to break free from them, sometimes we are unsure in which way we can communicate properly. As soon as one person starts opening up, it makes it easier and more comfortable for the other party to follow the lead. We need ice breakers to have deep conversations. A good conversation starts with sharing from your own perspective, your own feelings, and your own expectations. Talk about motivations and not positions. It's a little bit like getting naked first because it requires me to drop my layers of protection and show my vulnerabilities. In my experience, the other person is willing to open up much more if I go all-in first, and then subsequently, the conversations I engage in unfold on a much deeper level. I find it fascinating how well it works. Ultimately, this analysis process is not limited to moments in life where things go wrong. With friends, for example, you can have this type of intimate conversation to celebrate your friendship. With my close friends, I try to practice the pro-active celebration of joyful moments. So when we had a great evening together, we write to each other reaffirming our positive experience. Yes, I know, this sounds like something thirteen-year-old girls from the movies do, but I think it's very important for human well-being to find ways to verbalize our emotions and cultivate our relationships.

In a negative interaction, sometimes, my reactions are so strong, that I need to remove myself physically, for example by just walking away. I need to understand first, what causes my uncomfortable feeling, the feeling of being hurt, of feeling vulnerable, exposed to another person's judgment. This is my way of creating a little break and enough space for me to absorb and calm my feelings. I can then come back into the conversation with a fresh mindset and fresh energy. My current coping mechanism is something I call "instant forgiveness." Then I try to express my feelings in a way that is clearly framed on my individual experience. When feelings are hurt, there is no right or wrong. You cannot deny another person's feelings. It's a fact that my feelings are hurt, when I feel that they are hurt. It doesn't matter if your point is justified or not. So I am very clear in my communication about this. Most people, including myself, don't know when we hurt someone's feelings. It takes a little bit of reflection and boldness to speak about this. It's still a very tricky thing. So when I feel attacked, I try to forgive the other person for creating this feeling in me, not because I think they did something wrong, but purely because it makes me feel better, more empowered. So it's purely ego-driven, I admit it. The conversation that follows from this approach will not automatically resolve a fight, but it usually helps to foster understanding because I have transformed my communication. I'm still working on embodying this forgiving mindset in my interactions, now and then I still get very caught up in my emotional reactions. But I feel that it's important for me not to lose days of precious relationship time because I'm being stubborn or defensive. I have two kids, and in my interactions with them, we often speak about emotions. When I notice that they are upset, I share my observation with them and ask them how they feel. And then we speak about what made them feel that way. It seems that it helps to build a stronger relationship with them. Most of the time, we come to the conclusion that we feel frustrated because something didn't happen the way we wanted it to happen. And it's very important to feel the difference between frustration and anger that results from a situation where somebody used physical force against them. And of course, when they feel happy, we also try to understand the conditions that contribute to their feelings of elation.

How does this concept of human relationship relate to the workplace?

Work is all about relationships too. The relationships between employer and employee, between company and customer, between employees or across the entire hierarchy within a company are important for the well-being and performance of a company. In professional relationships, I try to communicate very clearly about my feelings when things don't go the way I had expected them to go. I actually don't think that it makes sense to compare people against each other. My view is that the willingness, the drive to keep learning and improving oneself is what makes an employee a great employee. Over time, people tend to only want to improve themselves if they feel that their work is appreciated. Ideally, all employees in the company feel motivated to contribute to our company goals and grow the company. When you love what you do, motivation is there. It's a basic, natural feeling.

What is the responsibility of a leader?

For me it's super simple: A leader makes the team better. To do this, I think a leader needs to pay attention to every single team member and cultivate motivation. He or she needs to be the one helping each team member be their best. They can do so by offering a new perspective, maybe a perspective they hadn't seen themselves and offer support for team members to grow. The nice byproduct is that if a leader helps you grow, you typically respect this person very much. This is where a relationship deepens. As a founder, my leaders in the business context, are my investors. They have a certain amount of power over my actions, and they have the duty to tell me when I'm doing something they believe to be wrong. I have respect for my investors, when they can make me aware of something I did wrong on a strategic or maybe even on a personal level. Ideally, they can even tell me what they think I could do differently rather than only pointing out the mistake. They should be open to listening to my version of the story. Only if they do so, can we align our goals.

What's your leadership style?

As a leader, I'm trying to create an environment that enables me to be authentic and live my life in a way that I find meaningful. We are a company, and we work hard, and yes, we do have our financial and growth goals. My aim is to meet people at the workplace every day who want to work there because it makes sense to them, and not because they are being told to work there. It should be an environment where vulnerability is okay. In any of these personality tests people use for leadership, I probably fare on the high openness degree. I try to cultivate a culture where we don't really have secrets. Numbers and so on, are all transparent as far as possible. That counts for feelings too. I don't hide from my employees how I feel about them. I'm by all accounts not known for being the people pleaser CEO, but I try to be fair and transparent in my communication. Interestingly, I have found that my leadership style is that of a benevolent dictator. This means that I listen to everybody's point of view and discuss a decision that is to be made with the relevant team members. When I listen to others, I do not distinguish between people's levels of seniority. I check their expertise though. So this means that an intern's view can be as important or even more relevant than a vice president's view if the intern has more expertise in that field.

I also listen carefully to the concerns that people voice. We do have team discussions, but usually I make the final decision. We have the "Disagree and Commit" strategy. When a decision has been made, I'd ask team members to show unconditional commitment to supporting the decision. I feel that as a company founder it's my role to keep the company on track and aligned with a long-term vision. It doesn't matter then if the other decision might have been the better one, we will all need to commit to making it work. I don't appreciate statements like "Hey, I told you so," because this is really not helpful for learning and teamwork. In the startup world, many projects and decisions can turn out to be the wrong ones, I'd say even up to twenty-five percent of our decisions turn out to be bad ideas, and it's much more important that we are all on one page and bold enough to take this risk. We want to create this culture where we are not punished for making wrong decisions, because ultimately, many decisions will be wrong anyway. Every failure is an opportunity to learn. The success of the entire company is more important than that of individual team members, so it's also a matter of mindset to learn how to let go of this view of wanting to be right.

How do you keep that balance in diversity of thoughts if you hire only people with similar mindsets?

One of the core principles we have in our company is the willingness to learn. These things always sound so generic and stupid. One of our values is that "every criticism as an opportunity to learn." It's like if you drive a car and somebody stops next to you or honks the horn, rolls down the window, and says: "you drive like an asshole!" Instead of yelling back at this person, let's try to figure out what is beneath that strong emotional reaction so we can learn and benefit. Not every person is very advanced and trained in precise information, so some of your clients may package information in a way that seems harsh to begin with but ultimately proves to be very useful in sharpening our services, our products. Sometimes, we end up in situations where clients even blame us for things we have no control over. Still, I find it important to listen and understand if there is something for us to learn from it. It's not only important to learn how to receive criticism, but also to learn how to provide feedback in a way that is helpful to the other person. So every interaction between human beings, irrespective of their relationship, can be a valuable source of information, but it doesn't have to be. It's important to listen and then decide how you want to deal with this feedback.

If you want to create a learning culture in a company, each member of the company needs to be open to criticism and willing to give feedback in a way that helps the other person grow. One of the things I find very helpful to identify this mindset is to be a very attentive listener to how they tell their stories. Ask about the events in their lives, and ask what they liked and disliked about these events. Pay attention to the mundane things, how they view regular events in their lives This can help you understand what brings joy to them and how they will interact with your own customers. We also ask for skills and expertise, but I find the cultural fit most relevant, so I will be the one leading these interviews, whereas the functional interviews can be led by our HR experts. I will also do our onboarding of new employees myself, because I find it important for new hires to understand the main motivations for us in founding the company. It's an emotional onboarding, and I want our employees to know that from day one that they are part of our joint journey.

How do you make decisions in your company?

Our company uses the scrum methodology, as I come from a programming background and have had good experiences with this approach. What I like about it is that it's very simple. Scrum meetings have a structured agenda. There are some nice features of this structured process. First, there is a "done" section, that shows what work has been finished. Sometimes we do things that do not necessarily turn into something tangible. Let's say, we want to enter a new market, and a team member does the market analysis. The person spent the entire week analyzing the market, only to reach the conclusion that we should not enter the market because certain market conditions are not ideal for us. In a scrum meeting, this person has the opportunity to present this information and also state the conclusion. Other members of the team can learn from her thinking process. In regular meetings, we typically have the tendency to communicate only what went well, and in this case, it would look like this person hadn't done anything for an entire week, which is not the case! In start-ups, around half of the work done will not turn into something tangible because there is a lot of trial and error. If we forget to also appreciate this work that didn't result in anything, we degrade the efforts that were put into it, and we lose motivation. Second, sharing information across the team helps everybody in the team to be able to contribute. Every team member briefly explains what they are working on, how they are going to do it, and everybody can contribute their knowledge.

Last but not least, I find it very helpful to stick to what is to be done instead of engaging in endless strategy discussions. We have separate strategy meetings if we need to make strategic decisions. In every single team we have weekly sprint meetings, where we sit together and discuss what we did last week, what we plan to do this week, and why we are doing what we are doing. It's our opportunity to give immediate and caring feedback when we see that something can be improved so that we remain flexible. Every person has equal rights to point out something sub-optimal, and we try to do so in a way that doesn't make the other person feel bad and rather inspires them to grow. If this process goes well, the person who receives the criticism or feedback is thankful! In the driver example, I'd love our employees to not say "Hey, you drive like an asshole", but something like "Hey, when you passed the lane, I nearly crashed into you because I didn't see you coming! I think you didn't put on your blinker!" Typically, when we learn driving, we pay driving teachers to tell us that. How cool is it that we can get free advice all the time when we just learn to open up to criticism. There are so many things we don't know about ourselves, but other people around us can help us view ourselves more wholly. The only way of finding out is communication, but this communication is a skill. We need to practice that so that it becomes a mindset. The mindset to see feedback as a tool, to help people see how they can become better versions of themselves.

How do you as an organization learn from failures?

Again, I come back to the benefits of scrum methodology. The "*done*" section of the agenda is helpful because team members tell all the facts, and that includes also sharing what went wrong. We also speak about our feelings. Once the first person gets naked in terms of dropping their emotional shields, it's not that difficult for the others to follow the lead. I don't mind sharing with the team what I did wrong and what happened as a result of it or what I think I and we as a company can learn from this. It's very interesting to observe sales meetings. In general, sales people tend to be the ones who communicate very positively, everything is always great, and the huge deal is just around the corner. We do it differently. Everybody has to tell one story of what went horribly wrong last week. I find this so much more meaningful than just sharing success stories. I actually think it's quite cool if we can be proud of our mistakes and of course the learnings we draw from them. It's very important not to punish people for making mistakes, so that they will not be afraid of sharing them and start blaming external conditions for what happened. The only thing that makes me slightly angry is when people repeatedly do the same thing wrong because I think it's insane to keep doing the same thing over and over again and expecting different results to come out of it.

What should one look for in choosing the right investors?

Again, I think this is a very personal thing. I have founded many companies, some worked, some didn't work. In the beginning, I chose my investors by who paid the highest price or even who was the first to say yes. I'm not sure if I could have chosen differently because in the very beginning, often, you don't have many options, sometimes you only have one option.

However, when you have a little bit of a track record or you have different options, this is what I can advise: Ask what skills or assets they can bring into the company to help with the current stage. Have they already invested in companies that were at this stage? Do they already have some expertise in the market or product this company is in? So for example, while business angels might be a good source of investment in the early stages, still look out for additional dimensions of fit. In case you want to develop a neural network, ask yourself if you'd really want to have a specific type of person invested in your company. It's not only about the money, it's also about the opportunity to receive qualified feedback and access to a network. Investors need to have a little bit of understanding of the development stage that your company is in, in order to give qualified advice. At early stages, it's quite typical that almost everything goes wrong until one thing goes right. An inexperienced business angel might not even be a good fit for the very early stage because they might get super nervous when things go wrong and then ask you to do things that don't make sense. I find it quite important to do reference calls, that is, to call other companies that the investor has invested in and ask them what their experience in the interactions with the investor was like. Entrepreneurs are mostly willing to help other entrepreneurs, so you can mostly rely on their answers.

What do you want to share with the world?

We have probably come across the saying *carpe diem* a few million times. We may laugh about it, but I believe it's very much worth reflecting on simple sayings like these. Do spend a little bit of time and relate them to yourself, so that you can touch upon their deeper meaning. This is what I call the study of basic understanding. There is a big difference between knowing something and understanding something. For a long time, I had jumped over these simple truths, but I learned recently that basic things and their meanings are so much more helpful to understanding life and also we need to understand these basic things to be able to understand more complex topics. I try to reflect upon it in a structured way, step by step. When somebody had told me at age twenty about *carpe diem*, I would have come to completely different conclusions. For me, *carpe diem* is having breakfast with my kids, then taking them to school without being stressed. This means, I can't have meetings at 8:30 in the morning. Then, I try to spend my time in a way that I find worthy of a life. For me, this means a day that has plenty of opportunities to learn. It took a very long time to understand the way I want to learn. In retrospect I think I've spent way too little time reflecting on these basic questions in my early life. So it's very simple advice, but I think it's the piece of advice I would have loved somebody to tell me when I was twenty.

One last thing, that I want to share: Recently, I have started to expose myself to people who have very contrary belief systems to mine, and in particular I have started to engage with people who have extreme political views to which I would completely disagree with. I think the world is full of people running around telling facts. Everybody tries to sell their opinions as facts, and instead of listening to each other, most people spend their time convincing each other about truths. All we know is that we actually can't prove anything! There is no proof in this world! We can only disprove things and that means that there are no such things as facts, only opinions that haven't been disproved. While in science this may be useful, for life, it's important to understand that what I believe in this current moment can be completely different in five years. Bringing this to your mind when engaging in discussions can transform discussions into conversations because it helps you appreciate the opinions of other people. We are humans; we all have opinions. We can disagree with an opinion and still appreciate the other person. What I try to understand is what is beneath their personal views and what makes them believe that way. Emotions that pop up during these conversations are a rich source of data. So my little secret of intervention is changing the process in which I interact, and not trying to change the other person's mind. I'm tired of fighting about positions. I wonder if we can build more bridges by understanding what makes us act in a certain way. What feelings or emotions are the driving factors, and what is the deeper motivation of raising your voice to say things in the way we say them. And very often, when I listen on this deeper level, all of a sudden, I can feel a relationship with this person because I can relate to their feelings, their concerns. It's a very powerful insight from my relationship building practice.

Beautiful brains change tomorrow...today
Brain-brush reflection exercise:

How did I feel when I read this?

What did I learn?

What will I integrate into my daily life?

Cybersecurity: An ode to human irrationality

Karsten Nohl,
founder and chief scientist of Security Research Labs

What fascinates you?

Hacking. In my team, we do hacking research, which means that we look for security problems in all kinds of technical equipment: computers, phones, critical public infrastructure, payment systems, and so on. It may sound technical, but I find information security is of high relevance to our society. Security is an arms race that determines how quickly we are willing to adopt future technologies. In this arms race, I'm equal parts excited and afraid about whatever problem we solve next. Because solving a problem on the defensive side usually leads to innovation on the offensive side too. For instance, in our field, we can use artificial intelligence to detect a hacking attack and react to it within milliseconds. It's an automated process. But imagine the hacker can also use AI that hacks systems at the same speed. This means, we exponentially increase the number of systems that are hacked. It's a curse and a blessing, and I don't think there are any foreseeable breakthroughs that would give one side a clear advantage. It's a cat and mouse game, and it's a game that can never really be won by either side. This constant fear of being hacked slows down innovation. Imagine if people were not afraid of being hacked and just accepted the risk of being hacked as something like a tax on the proliferation of information and digital revenues? We would create much wealth, and loose a small fraction of this newfound wealth to criminal hackers. Giving people this warm feeling about new technology, and at the same time keeping the data and money losses to a minimum, is my job.

What is the biggest societal risk from hacking?

Hacking becomes most damaging when it targets critical infrastructure. Technology-wise, taking down critical infrastructure is entirely possible. Electrical grids are just combinations of computers. There are many little vulnerabilities in the existing systems. Combining them often provides a relatively straightforward way to switch off the lights somewhere in the world, potentially for an extended period of time. Imagine somebody hacked into a large wind or solar farm and sending an overdose of electricity through the grid targeted at the next substation. An entire region would lose electricity for a day or longer. Very quickly, fresh food can't be kept fresh. Supermarkets would stop working because, even if they still had food, they couldn't sell it anymore for the lack of functioning payment systems. Cities would soon destabilize. And even governments might have problems coordinating and getting the police officers and military to mobilize quickly enough, resulting in chaos in a matter of days. If hackers coordinate their efforts, they can take entire cities off the grid and blow up a larger transformation station. This kind of hacking of critical infrastructure hasn't happened yet on a large scale. There have been smaller attacks in East Ukraine, though, that show it's only a question of intent not of technical capability: As soon as someone wants to damage critical infrastructure, they can...

What has prevented a large scale hacking of critical infrastructure?

By and large, the risk of a large hacking attack against critical infrastructure is somewhere in the same category as nuclear weapons! You wouldn't want to be the first to start, but you do want to be prepared to hit back if you are attacked. China, for example, has proudly announced that it has a cybersecurity army with several hundred thousand hackers. Even Germany has built an offensive cyber capability. Infrastructure hacking could, with relatively little effort, create chaos to a degree that we haven't seen in Germany since the second world war. Adding to the threat is the fact that it doesn't take a sovereign nation to hack critical infrastructure. Non-state actors could just as well cause a lot of pain, but we wouldn't know how to find them and retaliate. I don't want to speculate about the reason why no one has caused this kind of mayhem yet, but I can rule out cost as the reason. Hacking critical infrastructure does not cost very much, especially if you just want to hit any major city somewhere in the western world.

What can the public sector do?

The calls for regulating the internet space are becoming louder, even in democracies. I think regulation can do relatively little to stop hackers. But regulation can be dangerous if it kills a technology too early — we might lose out on trillions because we were worried about losing billions. On a macroeconomic level, hacking is just one risk of many that you incur when betting on innovation. Defending oneself is important, but we should not stop technological innovation just because we fear cybersecurity risks. Instead, we need to find an acceptable level of pain and view it as a fractional tax on our future gains. From a private sector perspective, security investments are an important component of digitization. Economic losses caused by hacking are a cost of digitization. I think at the market equilibrium we will always have some level of internet security risk. So much security so that there is no hacking would be "cost prohibitive," whereas so little security that everything is hacked would be "innovation prohibitive." So the equilibrium point is somewhere in between, at a reasonably small, acceptable level of hacking. We just need to make sure that the benefits and the risks are balanced.

How about regulation that helps security innovation?

In my view it's difficult to create top-down, prescriptive incentives for innovation. I think the most important step in internet security is to be aware of risks. This gives you the freedom to decide whether or not you want to manage certain risks. It's not so different to the car industry. Just like we have improved car safety literally from the moment cars were invented, today, a hundred years later, people are still dying in car accidents. My colleagues and I at SRLabs recently did a scan of the entire internet to understand the security landscape and the impact of regulation on protection across industries and companies. In the banking industry, we found that European entities, which are highly regulated, performed significantly better on absolute levels in areas in which they were regulated, such as identity management or server performance. However, in other areas that had not been in the scope of regulatory requirements, they performed much worse — this may be an indication toward companies' lack of incentive to go the extra mile. Companies stop investment in areas that are regulated once they meet the requirements. But in cybersecurity, the "weakest link" principle is important. It doesn't matter where you are strong because it matters more where you are weak. And it seems that strong regulation unintentionally weakens banks. We definitely never will have enough people to address all vulnerabilities — there are more and more people coming into the sector, and at the same time, demand for skilled talent is growing exponentially. This should not prevent us from having a public discussion on the time and budget discussion to bring more people into the internet security business.

What seems to improve security to some degree is to force companies to publicly disclose breaches, so as to make it embarrassing for them. If you get hacked, you have to tell everybody about it and you can't hide it. Sometimes, hacking is a cost incurred due to gross negligence. And the risk of public shaming seems to be working more effectively as it leaves the decision with the companies as to how they want to secure themselves. It's such a new and super fast evolving field, and as we all know, universities are also not very capable in teaching this. How could professors, who've been teaching for twenty years, know much about present-day internet security? Where would they have gained relevant, real-world experience? We need to bring people closer to the essence of technology to understand how it works. In Israel, for example, there is mandatory military service for everybody for three years. That's actually the length of an undergraduate degree, so that's basically a full education. Every year, a large number of people graduate from the cybersecurity teams in the Israeli military and enter the private sector. I'm not suggesting that countries should bump up the military to educate their citizens about cybersecurity. Nevertheless, it is an important strategic asset for a nation. The US is doing a good job by outsourcing a lot of large security efforts to private companies. This means that you don't have to work for the government to gain experience in high-level cybersecurity. Edward Snowden, for instance, didn't work for the government. He was a subcontractor working for the National Security Agency. Well, in this case it didn't work out for the government as intended, but from a macro-economic point of view, this is how knowledge is dispersed into the industry. In particular because in the private sector you change jobs every once in a while. In Germany, we don't have these dynamics, and people who work in cybersecurity for the government typically work there forever.

What else do you want to share with the world?

For people like me, who are engineers, analysts, and rational thinkers, it is very challenging to navigate the world of humans that seems to be so irrational. I have always been fascinated by psychology and, in particular, behavioral economics. A finding from this field of research is that people are more afraid of losses than they value gains. If I give you something and take it back right away, you're more sad than you were in the beginning even though you didn't really lose anything. We are in a lucky position nowadays, where we can use technology to support our personal growth. Already twenty years ago, when you went online, you could possibly consume more information than you would be able to process in your entire lifetime. However, twenty years ago, it was considered quite unpopular and nerdy to go online and seek guidance on a topic of your choice. Nowadays, it's quite normal for people from all walks of life to use Google to seek advice for professional networking or planning your private life. This shift in societal acceptance of the internet opens up many possibilities for us to become who we want to become because it's okay now to go online and find your virtual mentor or teacher. I've tried so many times to understand human behavior, and whenever I believe I have understood, I find myself being completely dazzled again by the outcome of a meeting at work or an election in a country. Maybe we need to think about models in which the optimal, rational outcome is a balance between fears and joys. So what I'd really want to learn is to view the world through a pair of human glasses. Is there any training where you can learn to adjust your definition of rationality so as to reconcile rationality and irrationality? I'd love to be able to acknowledge deep-rooted anxieties around change or loss and not find myself dumbfounded at the irrationality of behavior over and over again every time I encounter human decision making. It's so important to me, because, in the end, society, democracy, corporations, even family, are all human systems. In these systems decisions are made by people, not by machines. And we humans are full of heart, full of fear, full of joy, right?

Beautiful brains change tomorrow...today
Brain-brush reflection exercise:

How did I feel when I read this?

What did I learn?

What will I integrate into my daily life?

Healthcare 101: When empathy meets conviction

Veronika Schweighart, founder at Climedo Health

What is most fascinating to you currently?

I work in healthcare, and I'm driven by the desire to contribute to the advancement of personalized healthcare for patients. We live in a promising era where we have started to discover tremendous possibilities that technology and research into genomics have to offer our health system. We can personalize treatments based on the patient's DNA. Personalized treatments are much more effective than "one-size-fits-all" treatments and they can reduce side effects. I have a close family member who had leukemia when he was a child. Chemotherapy, the way we use it currently, is a one size fits all approach in which every patient gets a similar treatment regardless of their completely different physiological context. The chemotherapy destroys the cancer, and it destroys many other things in your body like your immune system as well. It's not precise, it cannot distinguish between good and bad cells. Sometimes patients are actually killed because of the chemotherapy and not because of the cancer. Fortunately, in my family member's case, the chemotherapy — despite all the unnecessary side effects — turned out fine, and he is well now. Having witnessed first hand how much pain the chemotherapy caused him, I am more thrilled and motivated to spend my time and energy working towards improving medical treatments.

What is the most pressing problem in healthcare?

In healthcare, there are many stakeholders. The most obvious stakeholder is the patient. While he or she should be the center of attention, this is not always the case. But there is a shift towards patient-centricity in the healthcare space, so the patient is now gaining significant power. Then you have the doctor or the medical professionals involved in the treatment of the patient. They operate in a hospital or small practice environment. You also have the provider of medicine or medical devices, which would be the private sector, that consists of pharma and the biotechnology companies. Medical treatment is by large paid for by insurances. These can be private companies or public institutions. And then you have the regulators, the public sector, who set the rules for the market and who are powerful in the healthcare industry. There are also technology providers like my company, who traditionally have not been considered part of the healthcare ecosystem. We build a new layer, something like an enabler layer to connect and integrate the main players in the field. It's not entirely new, because there have always been providers of technology in each of the different sub-industries, but we now have so many more opportunities to give this enabling function a super-boost thanks to advances in technology.

There is much cost pressure on all the players in the system. Many hospitals are in the red, and so they cannot procure the latest technology or implement the latest therapies. This is not only a big issue for them, but for the entire healthcare system and for governments because they are often publicly funded. So it's the taxpayer's problem as well. And the taxpayer is also the patient. Pharma and medical device companies are pressured from all sides to have effective and efficient ways to treat patients. And I think that the pharma industry is trying hard to find ways to leverage information technology and digitization effectively. Many of us have this view that pharma has held back innovations because they would lose revenue. At least in the case of personalized medicine, there is a clear win for the pharma industry. They can charge a lot for this: prices are around $475,000 per patient. They say this price is driven by the high investment cost that go into research and development of the therapy. One major cost lever is the cost for clinical trials to demonstrate safety of a therapy in order to get approval to commercialize it. Technology can reduce this cost for clinical trials. In addition, we see that business models in the industry are shifting from cost-based pricing to value-based pricing. Insurance companies or public payers want to optimize more for effectiveness of treatment rather than to pay per pill. This means if we can prove the case that personalized medicine is more effective than conventional methods and if we can reduce costs of clinical trials through use of technology, there is a win win for the entire ecosystem.

In my view, the largest pain point in this highly dynamic and complex ecosystem is insufficient collaboration and lack of exchange of crucial information which would be needed to give a patient the best treatment needed. The industry is very far behind in terms of digitization: documentation and exchange is still mostly via paper, fax or telephone! And along the long communication chains between this multitude of stakeholders, information is lost, or there are errors in transmission of the information or it just takes ages for information to reach the recipient. It's a structural flaw that prevents information flow to the detriment of transparency and patient well-being. The patient suffers most because he or she does not get the treatment in the right time. Sometimes it takes several days to find a sample in a lab! Just imagine how long it takes for labs and hospitals to transfer information when institutions are in different locations and don't belong to the same legal entity. Communication is crucial for the effectiveness of collaboration across teams and entities. It's not rocket science to solve this problem with all the technology and data processing capabilities we have today. In our globalized, internet-enabled world, reviews and reputation have a stronger impact than ever. Thought leadership in social innovation may end up being the game changer. So I think there's hope, and yes, maybe I'm a bit naive but that's just how I see the market dynamics.

What are roadblocks for personalized medicine to become a large scale intervention?

In summer 2016, the first immunotherapy called "Car-T-Cell" therapy was approved by the US drug administration. This was a big breakthrough for personalized medicine! Car-T-Cell therapy is a cancer therapy completely personalized to your genome material and it's making use of our own immune system to fight cancer by genetically modifying our immune cells. We have white blood cells, so-called T-Cells, that can recognize and destroy cancer cells. In the personalized medicine approach, these cells from the patient will be enriched with antigen receptor proteins, the so-called CAR, which help them go on a targeted search to eliminate specific cancer cells. The risk is your immune system suddenly goes crazy because it may be overwhelmed by its super power to seeing all these cancer cells it hadn't seen before, but there are great hopes to this new therapy after recent studies and trials had shown a cure rate of over 80% for patients who had tried other therapies without success. Overall, I think there are two main roadblocks to scaling this therapy, and they hold for the healthcare industry in general: One is we still need to show the proof of concept on a large scale. There are no longitudinal studies because this therapy is just too recent. For the moment, we have a proof of concept only for simple single tests. We cannot tell yet if certain approaches to personalized medicine approach are the most effective ways of treatment, it's just a hypothesis. Second, we also need to build societal trust and acceptance for personalized medicine. Personalized therapies require the collection of a vast amount of personal data. Many people still have resistance to sharing their personal data. As a society, we need to create tools and policies that help people gain trust that their data is secure and will not be misused. In medicine, there is this fear that people's data will be shared with health insurance companies and that these companies will then deny access to treatments or increase premiums. To build trust, we need to show the benefits of sharing personal health data, the risks linked to it, and our technological, institutional and regulatory solutions to cope with these risks. Data security is important. What I think is at least equally important is to make tangible the societal costs of not sharing personal data. I think society has not understood yet how many people are actually losing their lives every day because we are too scared of sharing our personal data to validate the effectiveness of new treatment therapies.

What is your company's big vision and what problem are you solving?

In general, we envision a future where every patient can benefit from all data points and all the insights that patients before them had contributed so that we all can have access to the most effective therapies available on the market. If we can build something like a holistic medical database, patients can even get alerts if they are at risk for certain diseases. So they can do health checkups more often and thereby reduce their risk. What we want to see is a shift from focusing on curing diseases to promoting better health through prevention. Prevention is key and will become even more important in the future. To prevent diseases, first of all, we have to know the whole development of a certain disease. And that's why we are starting at the hospitals, and we work in making clinical trials more efficient to reduce the cost of personalized medicine through improving communication and data flow. Currently, there's a big window of opportunity in the clinical trial market because it is so far behind in terms of digital infrastructure. In contrast, the pace of innovation is high and daily there are new therapies that enter the market and need to be tested. So we have a big clash in supply and demand, and participants, in particular doctors, are actively searching for solutions to alleviate the pressure. A clinical trial is a complex process. In a typical clinical trial, there are many stakeholders. There is lots of data gathering involved, and this data is then processed by many different sites. Data entry is crucial.

Typically, data entry is done on paper. Doctors ask patients how they feel and so on, and then they write it down on paper. Then this paper is scanned, or just sent to another institution by fax, where it is then entered into some system. That's where double data entry happens for the first time. From there, data is captured in an electronic case report form, that is needed by the pharma companies and the respective monitors to validate the efficacy of a treatment. Often there is no communication interface, so the data would then be re-entered for the third time. Typically, each stakeholder participating in a clinical trial has their different data systems. They might enter different data points or have different wording for their data entry, and then they won't match along the process. This manual process is prone to errors because sometimes handwriting is unreadable. Therefore the data quality is often very bad. So by solving these little problems we can enhance data quality for the benefit of better outcomes. Digitizing and standardizing data entry is a big part of the solution for future medicine. It's not only good for patients who need to re-enter the same data every time they go to a hospital for a checkup. Pharma companies and the involved service providers are also interested in faster processes and enough data points and high quality data to then decide if the medicine is ready to enter the market or not, or to get to the next level of clinical trials. There are some early adopter hospitals who are experimenting with digital communication interfaces, but the major players in the clinical trial market have not yet digitized their processes.

Our company was started with trying to understand the problem landscape with the mission to improve healthcare with the power of digital technology. The key person in the clinical trial system are the doctors because they are the ones who implement the trials with their patients. They need to test those new therapies in a heavily regulated environment. They need to collaborate with other doctors and with labs and with the drug companies and so on. We wanted to help those who have a direct impact on the patient and whose impact could be multiplied if they had the right tools. We decided not to position ourselves in the pharma market because there were already so many technological players. It makes sense — these companies have the highest budget to source products and services. It's also a value-driven decision: We found it's unfair the way the market is structured. People in university hospitals earn way less than any other player in the industry, and it's just so because they are mainly funded by the state. Early in our market research process, we inspired one of the medical doctors at Charité University Hospital in Berlin to become our medical advisor. We didn't stop right after finding a first partner. We wanted to see if the problem scope we had identified would also hold true for other university hospitals. Was this a common problem with a market large enough to provide for a company? We did not want to become this small fish providing a customized solution to one player and then become irrelevant for the industry. We interviewed over 100 doctors from university hospitals and when we were convinced the problem was big enough, we started to do rapid prototyping to create a solution making doctors' and nurses' everyday lives at work easier. We equip the doctors with digital tools that help them have a better overview of what is happening with the patients. With our software, they only need to fill in the data once, and they can immediately transfer relevant data to the next instance in the process by one click. It sounds simple, but filtering out the right data set in an environment where you need to monitor lots of data is a big value-add. This increases transparency and therefore makes the clinical trial much more efficient and more secure.

What have you learned from running startups?

There is this saying that if there's a possibility for ten-fold improvement to the status quo, people will be willing to change their behavior. Or the pain they are suffering in their everyday work must be so big that they think whatever will help a little bit is worth a try. To be successful, you need lead users who are early adopters. Start small, with a pilot customer. In our case, we started with two doctors and their research group. We created logins for them, and then we tracked the adoption patterns. We monitored closely in which way they used our technology so that we could develop the features and functionality in a way most helpful to them. Having a user-friendly interface is key for adoption, and it's a key competitive advantage in an industry like healthcare where most of the applications are not user-friendly at all. They gave us regular feedback on what needed to be improved. They used it because it made their lives easier. I think by engaging closely with the doctors in the development process, they developed this sense of ownership for our technology. It was not only our baby, it was also their baby. And they were proud to show it to others, and this drove early adoption rates and helped us to get paying customers early in the process. In health technology, you typically have lengthy sales cycles of twelve to eighteen months. In Germany, the IT departments in hospitals are rigid, and it takes ages to convince them to set up a new service because they do not want to install too many applications. We addressed this issue by offering a secure cloud solution. I think if you make it in Germany with data security, you can make it everywhere. With our approach, we reduced the sales cycles to an average of five months. So that was a great breakthrough to us.

When we interviewed the doctors, we asked them how much they could afford to pay. A little bit later in the process we found out that the situation was a little bit more tricky. Most of the studies were paid for by grants that hospitals received from different sources of funding, and this complicated things. In the heavily regulated and highly bureaucratic healthcare funding landscape, every little investment needs to be explained thoroughly. You have to provide a clear value-add if you want to justify expenses for a new software solution. The way we solve this problem is we just become part of the grant structure. So instead of monetizing from hospitals, we are monetizing from public grant schemes or the study sponsors from industry like pharma companies. It's a different business model, and it needed some rethinking and experimentation, but I guess in entrepreneurship, it's important to go with the flow.

On a more personal side, I think a well functioning team is the biggest driver in a startup. Team building and people development are therefore important skill sets. The moment of truth comes when you have bad times with your team. In my first startup, we had built a dream team of a computer scientist, a UX designer, and myself coming from the business administration side. We had met during an intense one-week boot camp for building new ideas at our university. It seemed perfect, and after some initial pivots we were quickly funded and acquired 20,000 users for our software within only eighteen months. But while we had similar value systems, and our long term vision was clear, we had different ideas on the way to get there. We tried hard to stand together, but it was impossible to make strategic decisions that made sense to all three of us. Discussions went back and forth to a point where we were unable to move forward. We just reached a plateau and were paralyzed. We even asked a professional mediator to come and help us overcome our conflicts. We analyzed from different positions and in the end, we decided it made sense to go separate ways. It was one of the toughest decisions in my life because the company was like my little baby. So in the end, I left the company as a managing director and my two co-founders continued the journey.

How do you keep a well-functioning and happy team?

In my view, it's more art than science. It won't help to choose a team only by hard facts because from the outside and on paper everything can look perfect. But if the communication and everyday interaction is bad, the team is doomed to fail when there are real problems to be solved. One way to not let crisis be a litmus test to your team is to do regular feedback sessions in which you need to be honest and open about your feelings. Have these honest and empathic conversations at least once a month so that you can let go of everything that might get in the way at a later point. In this way, you can build trust and trust helps speak about topics that are otherwise difficult to address. Ideally, you can still leave the room as friends even when you have tense discussions. It is in these moments of tension that we show the range of our personalities. Being yourself means being yourself without any compromise. And when you can be yourself, you can solve conflicts quickly. There are many conflicts, when you work in a field that you are passionate about. We are young, and each of us brings much energy, and we care a lot about our individual contributions to our company. We have high levels of self-confidence, and we have strong opinions because we are so enthusiastic.

It's important to have clear topic ownership allocation and to respect each other's expertise and decision choices. It's not necessary that we discuss each decision with everyone in the team because we trust the expertise and decision-making of the other person. We also trust if we see any problems, the topic owner will be open for feedback and not shy away from working out a solution that takes into consideration our feedback. In the end, we still give each other the authority to make their decision. Of course sometimes we make decisions that turn out to not be wise decisions, but at least we made a decision. We prefer to go forward and make 100 mistakes because in moving you also accumulate experience. Mistakes are part of learning, and the more mistakes you make, the more you learn. So many things don't work out, daily, but it's just good to learn from these things that do not work out. If you don't try, you will never know if they work or not. When you try to solve a problem, a risk free way to learn a lot in a short amount of time is by talking to people from different backgrounds and different industries. Gather their differing opinions, listen, don't come with a script. There is so much to learn from others. And it's also a fun way to learn because people typically have interesting stories to tell when you care about what they do and how they lead their teams. Listening to diverse opinions before making a strategic decision is important, hence I am a strong proponent of diversity in teams. It goes beyond gender equality. We also need to embrace diversity in skill sets, in culture, in perspectives, and in age. And last but not least we need a lot of empathy so that information can flow and collaboration works smoothly.

Anything else you want to share with the reader?

With my four-years experience as a full-time entrepreneur, I can already summarize that it is extremely fulfilling to start your own venture, despite — or probably because of — all the ups and downs. My personal mission is to help more people, especially women as they are still underrepresented in this field, to find the courage to become entrepreneurs. Recently I coached a student, and I asked her if she could imagine starting her own company. She said that she was too scared to do so, and she said so in a sad tone. I always wonder why people are so afraid of becoming entrepreneurs. It's such a rewarding journey from which you can learn so many useful things about yourself and about how the world works. I grow so much with our company. Every day I have at least one situation where in retrospect I feel like "wow, I learned so much." It's either from a conversation or an interaction with a team member or from any interaction with our stakeholders like our customers, our investors, our business partners. If I don't learn from them in a technical way, I still learn so much about myself and my reaction to an interaction. It's a nice productivity life hack. My mission is to transfer all the knowledge, the experience that I have accumulated as a founder of a company to others who want to go on a similar path. I love to work with inspiring people, and I think there is some truth to the law of attraction. When you are inspirational, you attract inspirational talent. This is when work becomes meaningful and collaboration becomes fun, when each person is contributing their best and not scared of stepping out of their comfort zones.

I feel grateful to live in a society that has started to encourage young people to become entrepreneurs and where people with entrepreneurial experience are highly sought after in the corporate world. Entrepreneurship is no longer a risky life choice, it's a great adventure that pays off well even on your CV. In case you do not have access to any convincing opportunities for entrepreneurship around you, don't worry. There is always an opportunity to think with an entrepreneurial mind and start to shape your work life in a way that suits your preferences. Start small, be innovative, be courageous. Start owning your tasks, take on responsibility for little projects that matter to you, speak up if you don't like something. In this way, you can step by step create your own little empire even as an employee in a larger company, known as an intrapreneur. It doesn't take much space to build in some innovation into your daily work life. When you have the right intrinsic drive and passion, even little things can have big impact.

Beautiful brains change tomorrow...today
Brain-brush reflection exercise:

How did I feel when I read this?

What did I learn?

What will I integrate into my daily life?

Contemplation on a System Called Life... Not More, Not Less.

Cem Dinc,

doctoral student in medicine and former player of the Turkish national basketball team

What is currently most fascinating to you?

I am fascinated by the fact that life is a constant river of experiences, which you accumulate every day. We are so used to experiencing new things every day that we totally forget how fascinating even the most mundane things such as doing the laundry or meeting our own deadlines can be. I like asking myself "why" or "what is the meaning" of a life experience. The more I actually learn about life, the less I think I know. It does not actually matter that I have a hard time finding any satisfying answers to these questions. The process of inquiry is actually quite a joyful experience in itself. I feel that every answer is a little step that brings me closer towards participating in a bigger context of humankind. It is quite a blessing that I can learn from other people's experiences. Sometimes, I learn the coolest things from people who I randomly meet, from whom I would not expect to learn much, and still magic happens. Having a relaxed, beautiful and real conversation with a genuine person gives me goosebumps and be in awe of life. It is in these moments that I feel one human being is meeting another human being, and we can just be bare, the way we naturally are. When we can let life unfold with all its emotions, as it wants to be lived. My indicator for the quality of an experience is when we do not need to rationalize it but can embrace it the way it is, when there is no need to philosophize over an experience. I love sharing with people how I feel about our interactions, and I am curious about seeing what impact my thoughts have on others. It's not to make others or myself feel better, but instead to have a chance to learn from each other's feedback. In the past, receiving direct feedback was not always easy for me, and often times I felt an urge to rationalize it. Today, however, I feel like I can be aware of other people's thoughts without being judgmental. To put it in a nutshell: I am most fascinated by the magic of this deeply interconnected system called life, which I have not yet fully grasped. I have a lot of respect for people who practice humility and who are curious about understanding the interrelations of things, rather than just claiming that things work in a certain way. Commitment is important so that systems can perform effectively, but systems are also impermanent in their nature. In a system, actions and their effects are interdependent. For this reason, I think it is quite important to observe, to learn, and to try to understand the system dynamics that are within us and around us.

You played professional basketball for the Turkish and German national teams. How did you make your decision between the two?

I joined the German national basketball team at age fifteen. At that time, this was one of the greatest experiences of my life. When I watched basketball, I cheered for both the German and the Turkish teams. But there was always this fear of one day having to play against the Turkish team. When I expressed my feelings as a youngster, I lost the support of many people in the

German basketball network. As a teenager, I didn't really understand that professional basketball is a business. To me, it was what I loved doing most, and I thought of it simply as a game. From a business standpoint, voicing my sympathy for the Turkish team was not a very smart move at that stage of my development as a player. If I had been my own coach, I would have told my younger self to not think too much, and to not take emotions and belonging too seriously. I would have told myself to make one commitment and follow through. All this questioning and ruminating is of no good use when one is at that stage of development, although it is also part of the learning process and growing up, in general. At age twenty, I was playing for the Turkish A Team, which was a great honor and relief, in particular because I had fallen into disfavor with the German Basketball Federation. I remember the moment I wore the Turkish jersey for the first time, looking in the mirror, feeling tears in my eyes. My feelings were overwhelming. I was nervous and happy at the same time. I was proud and grateful to get this wonderful opportunity and to keep moving towards what I had dreamed of. I played for two more years, and after a series of injuries, I exited the professional basketball world. Life is a series of unpredictable events: I went from structuring my day around basketball to studying economics at Harvard University. After I finished my degree, I realized that I still hadn't reached where I wanted to be, and I decided to study medicine.

What brought you from basketball to medicine?

When I received my general qualification for university entrance, I had already been contemplating becoming a doctor after my basketball career. Moreover, my high school basketball coach in the United States once told me: "One day, the ball is going to stop bouncing." As a basketball player, I personally struggled with finding a purpose in what I was doing. As time passed, it became more challenging to assure myself that this was what I really wanted to do in the years to come. Medicine, on the other hand, is a path where I can see myself contributing in a way that makes sense to me without questioning my intentions. I really do not know if I will be able to live up to my own expectations. I try to keep my eyes and ears open because life always brings about opportunities. I'm not the only player in this circus of life, and I'm definitely not the one who sets the pace of the play. Life happens, and yes, I do have a voice, but I do not think that, within the context of a hypothetical bigger picture, my voice counts much. That's why I observe what is happening around me and inside me. I have been studying various subjects, but those reflections are my real studies. Things happen, and they make a lot of sense in the way they happen, so I continue to be observant.

Can you describe the healthcare system?

As a medical student, I have had the opportunity to gain work experience at various health facilities. But I have also been in health facilities as a patient. As a basketball player, for example, I had an injury that had kept me in the healthcare system for several months, and I was able to discover all the care and also all the limitations to the true potential of our healthcare system. A health facility, such as a hospital, is a system that is quite regulated. There are many rules, and organizations have established standard operating procedures for how things should be done, such as, if you have this indication, I can prescribe that medicine, and I have a given budget for certain interventions. This is quite helpful because it provides some stability to a system. Nevertheless, there are a lot of people from various layers of the healthcare system who are unhappy with their current situation, so I think about how the existing system can be improved. When I started to study medicine, I was very idealistic. I thought that I was becoming a doctor to find the solution for the patient's suffering. In medicine, as it is perceived in western countries, the prevailing view is that the ultimate success of a medical practitioner can be measured in healing a patient, in preserving life. But in the process of becoming a doctor life has taught me some humility. Unfortunately, or fortunately, things are not that simple. A doctor never brings healing to a patient all by himself. A patient who is only looking outside of themselves for healing will never find satisfaction. There can be some temporary relief, but ultimately, real satisfaction, true well-being, can only come if patient and doctor bring in their best intentions and have genuine conversations with both parties accepting and embracing the uncertainties of life.

My observation is that the existing healthcare system is not performing well in certain areas. For instance, the people involved are not very happy about it. This is a strong indicator for an existing need to rethink the current system. A game-changing optimization lever for healthcare providers is the atmosphere, the "aura" we can feel when we step foot into a hospital and whenever we interact with medical personnel. It is an individual experience. How often do patients feel they are entering into an oasis for well-being when they come to a hospital? It's absurd that we spend so little of our attention on making it a place where it feels safe to recover. It's a paradox. How is one supposed to recover properly if the conditions there make them feel even worse upon entering? And what about the staff who are spending their entire days and nights there? It isn't difficult to imagine that this is not where they will draw a lot of energy to bring their best performance into the medical care of patients.

Every time I think I have found a solution I find there are many more options if I keep on asking for the root causes. For instance, let's take a look at the education system that produces medical doctors. Doctors can use their medical knowledge and practical experience to elevate science to new frontiers. But our current system makes it very difficult for doctors to venture into new fields. The existing healthcare system trains people to let go of critical thinking and memorize certain prevalent views. It starts with the selection process of medical students. And it continues throughout the medical studies. Students are awarded good grades only when they learn things by heart and reproduce certain thinking patterns. This will not train them to question underlying assumptions that may produce growing opportunities for the prevailing system.

Can you visualize a different hospital system?

Ideally, a workplace should feel as natural as a home. When entering a hospital, there is a probability one needs to stay there for an extended period of time, so it might temporarily become home. How do you imagine your home? Wouldn't it be nice to feel warmth and love around you? A feeling that the hospital staff care about themselves and make this place their home, as well? Wouldn't it be humbling to see patients who are fully satisfied with their stay in the hospital bring thank you gifts to the staff? These would be moments of joy for everyone involved. Upon entering this place as a person seeking recovery, one should feel that they are in good hands. It doesn't take much to make a place feel more welcoming. The least we can do, as medical staff, is to welcome guests to our respective departments the way we would welcome guests to our homes. It doesn't cost anything; it's a matter of intention. At all times, we can signal that we care, and that we will do our best to listen and treat everyone as a human being, seeing their full essence. In the end, we are all humans who are equally valid, irrespective of whether we are a doctor or a patient.

How would you start transforming the healthcare system?

There need to be incentives for keeping a spirit of innovation, for creating an environment in which nobody is tempted to resist change. Change has to be part of an organizational culture, and change is part of human life anyway, so it would go well together. I find it particularly refreshing to learn from people who have worked in various organizations and several industries because they look at a challenge from a different perspective. Their analysis of a case differs based on their training and their expertise. And if old views and new visions were integrated, we would get a more holistic understanding. So ideally, we have rotational programs across departments, across organizations, and across disciplines. What keeps us from thinking that surgeons can learn from psychiatrists and vice versa? Physical healing and emotional healing processes have similar patterns. There is a huge learning potential. Cross-collaboration is far from reaching its peak. And that is not because it's impossible. Holistic understanding of human suffering has not been a focus of the healthcare system so far, and society has not asked for institutionalization of cross-disciplinary knowledge exchange forums. To put it bluntly: the market has not been entered yet.

One of the key skills of a coach is the ability of not just hearing the players but listening to them. When somebody listens to you skillfully, you feel not only their care, but you also feel their encouragement to make your own decisions. To know that you are not alone, to have somebody whom you may openly speak to. Growing up, to me this was my father. He was always a fountain of tranquility who gave me calmness and stability when I really needed it. That is a rare gift, and it's the essence of respectful interaction. Only oneself may know the answer to one's life questions. So as a doctor, the key role is listening to the patient, I believe. I had to learn to listen to others, and I am still learning. I observe developments that happen outside of my soul and outside of my body. Even outside of our own human systems we are embedded in a larger system and it is important to listen to each other. Patients who come to ask their doctors for advice should be observing themselves diligently. The doctor-patient relationship could be much more effective if patients were able to understand their own feelings, so they could verbalize them. If they cannot do so, they almost completely hand over the sovereignty of interpreting their suffering to the physician. Ideally, patients understand that doctors can only do so much. In the end, nobody knows their own suffering better than the patient. The better patients understand themselves, the more fruitful the relationship with medical personnel will be because it may grow from a genuine conversation between two authentic people.

What do you think about identity?

As a child, I never had a problem with identity until some artificial contrast was drawn. I grew up in Germany as the son of a Turkish father and a

German mother. There were times that I didn't feel I belonged. Today, when somebody asks me what I am, I just answer that I am Cem – no more, no less. We could get to know each other, and you may decide for yourself who I am to you. Identity can be an anchor for psychological safety, it can be a refuge, albeit I'd stress that, to me, it can only be a temporary solution. Human beings change. From one moment to another, you have already become another version of yourself. By the time we leave this conversation, we will have already changed into new versions of ourselves. As of now, you and I have already spent two hours with each other and some of your essence has left an imprint on me. Identity cannot be reduced to one single moment — it is the process of an ongoing inner conversation. Clearly, one cannot be in this reflection mode at all times. Nevertheless, I find it very beneficial to reflect how I feel in a certain moment, where I am headed, and if this is where I feel I should be headed. I appreciate checking in with myself. It is a process of becoming.

What else would you want to share with the world?

I feel very grateful to be part of this wonderful book because it offers a great platform for self-reflection. I would not hope for anyone to read this and outright think, "yes, he is right." I would feel more excited if someone eventually disagreed, only to start their own reflection process on their personal life journey. One may only live forward, yet looking backward is a way to shape the future so that what lies ahead of us becomes a journey worth embarking upon. Giving your full self to others is so much more valuable than giving something to them that you think they expect you to give or be. Giving people what they seemingly want is an impossible undertaking and makes things unnecessarily complicated. Ideally, we look at children and relearn how to be ourselves without pondering over outside expectations, how to let our emotions happen, and how to live them to the fullest. Then we may bring in our analytical, adult selves. Enjoying the reflection process is a noble activity in itself because if you have the privilege of knowing yourself you may do things that are good and true for yourself and at the same time beautiful to the world. I wish we spent more time listening to and not just entertaining ourselves, so that we may one day understand our value and all our possible contributions to this world. We have all it takes to be happy within us.

Beautiful brains change tomorrow...today
Brain-brush reflection exercise:

How did I feel when I read this?

What did I learn?

What will I integrate into my daily life?

Part Three:

How to Become Good Earthlings

Explore your intuition, and you can become a master

Edward Sizzerhand Obika, founder of sizzerbees and DJ/Producer at Square One

What fascinates you most?

There are many things that are happening in my life. Currently I'm working on a new music album, finishing my certification of professional beemastering, and on top of that I do have my regular job as an IT specialist in a corporation. And even if it may sound a little bit strange, I actually enjoy figuring out how to coordinate all these different building blocks of my life in a way that the whole is more than the sum of the parts. It feels like playing tetris, and my current mission is to place them in positions so that the entire game of life makes sense. Throughout the past decades I have constantly refined the different blocks. It took many years to build these products in the different areas of my life and bring them to a level of mastery that fulfills my own expectations. And there were some periods in my life where I really struggled to juggle all of them, to keep moving, mainly because they were so different in their nature. I have been a professional DJ for most of my life, and now it feels like I'm just at the verge of retirement in this field. I don't expect too many new opportunities to arise. But I look at this development with a sense of joy. Music has always been my love, and DJing has been my favorite hobby. Things in life just happen as they happen, the balancing happens by itself over the course of a lifetime. Now I'm at a point in my life where I can see everything come together nicely. It all makes sense in the big picture, finally!

What do you love most about DJing?

As a DJ, you create a space for the audience to experience something cool, something unique for other people in a given moment. It's a rewarding activity because sometimes people come to you after the show and tell you that they had a most amazing night thanks to your work. That's a cool compliment that you don't get too often in the stereotypical nine-to-five everyday work. I have always had a strong love for music. What I found really annoying when going to a club was to observe DJs who did a bad job. They maybe did not have the right technical skillset or didn't play the songs I wanted to hear. So I figured I just had to create the experience that I would enjoy myself. The most important skill for being a good DJ is your taste of music. It's not a magic talent, it's a skill that develops when you expose yourself to a variety of different music and invest some time into understanding where it comes from and in which way the styles differ from each other. It's something you can learn; it's quite technical. I had a music platform where we would review many different music releases. On top of that, as a DJ, you are also a live performer. It's important to observe the audience, to analyze their behavior. Over time you can just glance at the audience and intuitively get a good feeling for the segmentation. When I look at an audience, I can quickly estimate what share of the audience would prefer to listen to pop songs. Another share of the audience may prefer disco or funk. So then I need to adjust my settings to play the songs in a way that creates an experience where all of them can have a good time. The trick is that it's not about the individual song, but about how you put them together.

What did you learn from DJing?

In hindsight I think the central theme of my life has been to create something that is a masterpiece. I chose not to become a full-time professional DJ because when something is your profession, you sometimes have to find compromises. And for music, I was really not feeling that, and as long as it stayed a hobby, I could do whatever I wanted. It's quite cool if you get praise for your hobby, but because it's a hobby, it's just a hobby and this clear perspective has also been helpful in keeping my ego grounded in moments where my crew SquareOne and I were really successful and toured the world.

Throughout a DJ career, there are also some nights when the audience is not too appreciative. I try to draw my energy from the events that went really well. I look at my career as a series of events, and also here, I try to see if the bottom line was positive over the course of time. I think the biggest risk for DJs is that they limit themselves to one genre, and thereby deprive themselves of an opportunity. I think it's more helpful for your development if you start building a solid base in a genre of your choice, but then also look outside of the standard borders of the sector and find ways to enrich your portfolio. Whatever feels right to me and creates some joy in me is okay as long as it is also something that other people enjoy. By observing your audience closely, you can get better at understanding the audience. You need to pay good attention to see who will dance to what style of music, and then you need to make sure that you find ways to get the ones who haven't yet engaged with your music to start dancing too! Many DJ rookies fix their eyes on their screens, but then obviously they miss out on a wealth of relevant information! And when you watch closely, you can also do little experiments with new songs, new styles, and see the live feedback: People just stop dancing if they don't enjoy your set. It's not that dramatic if you get a few songs wrong every now and then, because a party lasts several hours and you have enough space to make up for some errors. There are always ups and downs throughout a night, and in my view, the bottom line of the entire experience is important, not the single song.

How did you move from DJing to bee mastering?

The technical answer is: I love creating cool experiences for other people. But to be very honest, it just struck me like lightning one day when I walked in the woods. I saw this beehive — buzzing, peaceful, just the perfect representation of nature. It felt like a calling, and I was intrigued to get my hands dirty and find out what this was all about. When I started, I really didn't think that one day I'd be mastering seventy bee colonies and writing a master thesis about bees. The first idea was that "hey, how cool would it be to own your own bees and give honey as a gift to loved ones." I started with three colonies. While I played around with the bees, I realized their importance for our environment. Fortunately for me, I live in a spacious old farmhouse in the suburbs of Munich that belongs to my grandparents so that I also have the conditions to play around and even scale the production. Along the way, I also received a lot of encouraging feedback from other people, in particular when I started to conduct little bee tours for local school children. Just the look in their eyes when they learn about the importance of bees is fascinating.

How are bees organized?

Bees live in a highly self-organized system. Most of the inhabitants of a bee colony are female bee workers. Each worker bee contributes to the maintenance of the bee colony according to her lifecycle stage. There are a few male bees, and there is a queen bee. This system has evolved over millions of evolutionary cycles, and it is quite optimized. Each bee knows what they have to do throughout their life cycle. The first few days of her life, a bee is a cleaning bee. Her anatomy wouldn't allow for her to do any other task. When her wax glands develop, she can contribute to building the home for the bees. It's quite cool to observe how bees build the little honeycombs in which they store their honey or the pollen. Until the twelfth day of life, a bee can't fly. Once she has reached a certain level of seniority, the bee becomes an explorer bee. She will explore the territory and find out where she will source supplies for the bee colony, before she becomes a guardian bee at the peak of her bee life. In this function, she will protect her bee family from intruders. After that, she becomes the collector bee and will use her skills to gather pollen and nectar from flowers. Bees have a very structured handover process, each bee knows exactly what her role in the system is.

What about the role of the queen bee?

A colony exists only if there are worker bees, drones, and a queen. If one of the elements is missing, the entire colony will die. If the worker bees realize that they do not have a queen, they panic. Instinctively they know that they are condemned to die. Bees that do not see a future for their bee colony, they become depressed and they turn into black bees and lose almost all their hair and die after a few days. When you see that a large share of your bee colony has this disease, most likely this bee colony will not make it through winter.

The queen bee is the one who secures the survival of the bees because she is the one who lays the eggs. Queen bees lay up to 2,000 eggs per day, and every day, many bees are born. You can actually see how experienced a queen bee is by the regulation skills she has. In the first year, the queen bee doesn't really understand yet how to interpret the data that comes in: she doesn't really understand how many bees she should produce based on the amount of honey there is in storage. You can really observe how she already adjusts the way she leads her colony in the second year. When queen bees get more experience, they can also venture out with half of the bee colony to build a new home.

A queen bee has the same genetic material as a regular worker bee. What determines if a queen bee or a worker bee is born from the egg is the food that is given to the egg. This means that even if a queen bee is killed, and there are still eggs available in a bee colony, they can always raise a new queen bee. The fascinating insight is that the food is what decides if they stay alive for five years or if they die after forty days. Queen bees receive what we call "royal jelly." It is produced in the gland in the head of the bees, and it is only for the queen bee. The cell, in which the queen bee egg lays, receives only this special food.

After around five years, the queen bee loses her productivity in egg production. The female worker bees realize this and decide that they need a new queen and they start to construct the cells for a new queen bee to be raised. They construct several cells so as to secure the option for several queen bees to grow. The current queen bee also contributes to building these new cells and by this she knows that her days are numbered. The first queen bee that hatches from the egg creates a very loud high-pitched buzzing. It's so loud that humans can hear it. All the other queen bees that are still inside their eggs will reply to this sound — they quack. And the new queen bee will come to the other queen eggs and kill each of them. It's the self-regulation of nature. What is even more fascinating is that there is something such as swarm intelligence, in a way that the bees will also wait until the new queen bee has mated before they get rid of the old queen bee. They don't kill the old queen bee, but the guardian bees will not let her enter into her home anymore. If the old queen bee tries to enter more than three or four times, she will be considered an enemy and be killed by the guardian bees.

What was your most interesting insight about bees?

Bees work in a system that is maybe not too distant from the human system. Let me share an example. When a collector bee has discovered a rich source of honey supply, she will take a sample and tell her colleagues at home about her discovery. Bees communicate with each other by dancing the coordinates of the source of food up to a level of detail of three to five millimeters. Not only do they communicate the coordinates, they also bring samples so the other bees can test the quality of the food. Some bees are just better at communication and others are less skilled. It is a little bit like a break dance party where you have a bee in the center dancing and nobody watches the dancer. And then you look again and everybody is watching. And each bee has their own strengths. The bee who is a terrible dancer might be a great builder. Some bees really suck at building honeycombs — you can see this when you look at the shape of the hexagons. And some of the guardian bees are not good at guarding their homes, they let everybody in. The beautiful part is that each of the bees has the chance to test all jobs during her lifetime.

What else do you want to share with the world?

There are things, that I really don't need, but I find them important to my life. For example, for my honey production business, sizzerbees, it's not too important if I have a certification as a master-level beekeeper. But to me personally, it's important, because going to school helps me acquire the knowledge that is important to fulfill my own quality expectations. And then there are many things in life where you can't really foresee when they will be needed. For example, now that I will have a certification, I may be able to commercialize products that I hadn't even been thinking of producing because I just didn't have the technical knowledge base to understand the full range of options available for product development. When you explore your intuition, you can become an expert in many different things. There are always some crossover effects as long as you build a thorough skill base in different areas. My IT job, for example, taught me how to build a good ecommerce store. The IT job is important to me because it keeps my intellect challenged. When I'm behind the DJ decks, I can combine my passion for technology and music and share my joy with others. To me, it feels wonderful to combine technical equipment with sounds and create beautiful experiences. With age, I have come to understand that what makes life a beautiful ride is the good mix of skills and passion. It's all connected.

Beautiful brains change tomorrow...today
Brain-brush reflection exercise:

How did I feel when I read this?

What did I learn?

What will I integrate into my daily life?

We need a new contract between society and nature

Dr. Martin R. Stuchtey,
founder and managing partner of SYSTEMIQ

What is the biggest problem that you're working to solve at this moment?

I'm trying to craft a small and humble contribution in answer to the question of how to reconcile economic and natural systems. I'm concerned about this whole question of how to rethink our economic system in a way that it provides just and sustainable outcomes for a 12-billion person planet. It's my little big thing that keeps me awake.

We've had an exceptional run of economic growth over the last 200 years since the early days of industrialization. Along the way, we were able to build material prosperity, improve our health, increase longevity and mobility. We have plenty of reasons to celebrate this stunning development. At the same time, we have reached a plateau. We are in a moment in history where we see stagnation in growth; as a matter of fact, we have grown poorer due to the tremendous costs in terms of natural resources that the powerful growth engine of our self-built economic system consumes. Everything in our economy is linked to resource consumption, and even our human well-being in the current system appears linked to consumption. In my view, the only way out is to massively decouple our notion of prosperity from economic growth. This means we need to decouple our human well-being from the amount of resources that we are using.

The good news is, thanks to progress in technology and business model innovations, that for the first time we can provide credible solutions to this problem. Thanks to affordable data analysis, for instance, we can now expand value creation from the pure selling of things to selling performance and outcomes. In addition, we are also experiencing some collective willingness to try out these new business models. I think we have developed a mindset, and a culture, in which we are starting to believe that decoupled growth could really happen!

How do well-being and prosperity relate to each other, in a decoupled world?

Let me first explain what I mean by decoupling. We need to decouple prosperity or well-being from economic growth; we need to decouple economic growth from resource use; and we need to decouple resource use from environmental impact. While we do need to solve the technical equation of the problem, we are looking for answers that are more profound. If we decouple prosperity from economic growth, and instead link it to the actual quality of our lives, we can actually feel prosperous when we do not grow economically. In this case, our well-being will not be hurt, even when traditional methods of economic analyses may find that we have grown poorer. It's about understanding, that we can live enriched lives, even when we do not grow materially. It's a bit ironic that societies only seem to recognize this relationship when they hit something like $30,000 gross per capita income. In other words, you'd need to be pretty rich and prosperous before you recognize there might be different drivers of well-being than growth-driven performance indicators. Most emerging economies have so strongly linked the notion of human well-being to economic growth that they are still optimizing for the latter at the expense of the former.

What would our economic system look like, if we managed to decouple economic growth from well-being?

I think it would allow us to make a major leap toward building an economy in which we are optimizing for gross contribution, rather than utility. There may have been moments in which this concept of the invisible hand, or the world of Milton Friedman, may have worked. In which we thought that as long as we optimized our own utilities, in aggregate, we would do fine.

In my view, this is completely unrealistic — serving our ego is not necessarily equal to serving society. We have seen over and over again that markets in which everyone is optimizing for their individual utility do not optimize for societal well-being. In our current economic system, the costs of our individual optimization actions are externalized, but that leads to reduction in societal well-being.

It feels like we are becoming more and more ungovernable. Governments are failing, and societies are falling apart. Things that we would have thought impossible three or four years ago are just becoming reality. Brexit, for instance, is a major driver of chaos and of wealth destruction. It kills opportunities for people, and with it, we lose security. We are winding back 70 years of European integration at lightning speed. I'm really concerned this will take us back to our worst historic hours.

Currently, it seems that autocratic models are better suited to managing the transformation necessary to cope with the challenges we face as humanity. They seemingly provide a clear strategic vision, and strong governance and leadership that follows up in action. A couple of countries seem to be falling prey to this oversimplified view of the world… I think it's a real threat to democracy.

We need to set up and govern our institutions in a way in which we measure their contribution, not only their profits. In my view, optimizing for shareholders only is insufficient. This is a trap that so many companies have fallen into. They maximize the value to something completely alienated from a human system.

You can't run a bank just to pursue a 15% ROI without answering the question: What is your bank contributing to society? This can be something as simple as "providing credit to entrepreneurs" so that they can build necessary solutions to cater to society's needs.

In a nutshell, we need to create spaces or economic systems in which people can produce a new product called contribution, and where the reward for this contribution is recognition, connection, a sense of shared identity. In our company, we try to design the architecture and facilitate the building of communities for change. Let's take the energy sector as an example. We bring together stakeholders from the entire value chain of energy, irrespective of the industry they are associated with. They can be from the IT industry, infrastructure, materials, the mobility sector. Oddly enough, sometimes, when we approach them, they tell us that they hadn't even been aware that they were part of the energy ecosystem. Through linking all relevant players into a new community, we can tap into a whole new world with different operating models, new technologies, and new sources of capital.

How do you bring about this new value-chain redesign?

First, there is the theory of case, which requires that you convince yourself and others that the current economic trajectory won't work anymore. For instance, it's not that difficult to show where global warming will take us. In Western Europe, we live next to a wonderful continent called Africa — and if we don't help prevent climate change, we won't be able to complain when our neighbors come to us because we have done nothing to prevent a climate crisis! It's not about creating panic, it's more about awareness.

I think there are many good examples we can leverage to help people understand the consequences. In fact, the Club of Rome and other organizations have already provided some base narratives about the limits of growth; there have been many wake-up calls.

What is more important is that we also need to help people understand there's a better alternative to the status quo, and that this alternative is achievable. For instance, the circular economy concept has demonstrated how we can recycle resources in a closed loop system. And what is more beautiful is: we can do so without compromise on the quality of the products generated in these systems. All we need to do is critically evaluate and adopt or maybe design new business models that can support these new economic opportunities, that come from regenerative low carbon business systems. Obviously, you need to have done your homework, and have a credible business case to underline your position. If we do this exercise well, people won't walk away from the truth because we can show them what they can move toward. We have a clear vision, an operating strategy, and tools to enact this envisioned system.

The second thing you need is a theory of change. We need to be thoughtful about where we can find the energy needed to fuel the movement of transformation. We can look at potential tipping points that are powerful enough to create paradigm shifts, because the alternative is social upheaval. History has beautiful examples — you can look into questions like: What was the start of the end of slavery? What was the start of the end of the exclusion of women from voting rights? When did Indonesians start wearing helmets on motorbikes? The answers to these questions give you a hint as to where you can mobilize enough resources to keep the revolution going.

And third, there is the theory of catalyst. This is linked to the understanding that time and resources matter. We can't do everything at once, but we can start with interventions that have a catalyst effect within our system.

Can you give us specific examples where this has already worked?

We are far from having redesigned an entire value-chain on a large scale. Let me share an example from the plastic packaging industry, which I find intriguing because you can actually see real progress in a short time.

Currently, we have many unhappy players in the ecosystem. Fishermen cannot fish because there is too much plastic in the way of the propellers of their boats — the quality of the fish is also a problem. Beaches are full of plastic garbage. Children cannot breathe because there is pollution from burning plastics. The industry has recently come under much social and governmental pressure for producing hundreds of millions of tons of plastic yearly without providing clear solutions on how to deal with the waste that ends up in our ecosystem. And customers and governments are putting more and more pressure on companies to stop polluting our oceans.

Why has this problem not been solved so far?

Because it's a complex problem that requires a holistic solution. So far, there has not been anything like a plastic recovery system that would pay for itself because we have looked at it from an isolated perspective. For instance, collecting plastic doesn't pay because there is no reward for recycling. Companies only reduce CO_2 because the consequence of not doing so is a fine, not because they see a feasible way to make use of the economic opportunity behind avoiding it. It's the same for households. It's not that communities in affected areas would be resistant to paying for a system that keeps their beaches clean and that brings tourists back. They just do not necessarily have the funds to set up this system for themselves. Companies would not be reluctant to pay a fair share in reducing plastic if there is a way to do so affordably. And on top of that, they would also be willing to pay a certain amount for reducing the CO_2 pollution that comes with the burning of polymers. If you add up all these little contributions that the different players in the market are willing to make, you may have enough resources to pay for an entire new system. Our company is basically the system enabling entity in the market. We bring together the right people to build this system.

Our team calculated that in 2020, we will have a ratio of three kilograms of fish to one kilogram of plastic in the ocean. In 2030, the ratio will be 1:1. We also had — this was when I was still at McKinsey — published reports about what a New Plastics Economy could look like. This was the new narrative for our theory of case.

The way we put the theory of change into practice was to convince a couple of brand leaders, that together made up around 10% of global volume, to adopt the "new normal" in a New Plastics Economy. Their commitment was a breakthrough for us to demonstrate a new paradigm in the plastic packaging industry. The message is: You can't afford to not use recycled materials! Then, in Bali, in October 2018, 290 institutions, led by the Ellen MacArthur Foundation, agreed to sign a commitment that by 2025 they would use 100% recycled materials, and, depending on each company, up to 40% of recycled content. As we speak today, in January 2019, we have more than 500 signatures already and more than 20% of global volume addressed. Still, this wouldn't be enough to move the needle if we couldn't implement it on the grass roots or community level.

So we established a program called "PROJECT STOP" (Stop Ocean Plastics) that aims at delivering the proof of concept of this New Plastic Economy. For this, we have won the support of large players like Borealis, Nestlé, the government of Norway, and many more. We would like to show that in five years, cities of 150,000 people and up to several million people can become plastic free. Not by coercion through the government, not by cleaning up overnight, which is only a short term solution, but by a transformation of the value chain into a New Plastic Economy. This shift can only happen in collaboration with all relevant players in this ecosystem, and by creating economic opportunities for anybody who is part of the system.

This can go as far as finding ways to empower waste pickers. Nowadays, they have smartphones in their pockets, which allows them to become something like Uber drivers for waste. For instance, they can trade their collected plastic into a certified supply chain so that they can be part of the economy. The owners of these recycling stations, the Nestlés and the Danones of this world, they can then recycle materials and live up to the environmental promises they have given to the world, to their customers, and to governments.

In the beginning, it's all about demonstrating that these little interventions can work out in practice. You can show that there is something to gain from the economics — one, you protect your brand from reputational risks, and secondly, you have just discovered a secondary access to resources. You would have, for example, corporations redesigning their packages in a way that they can be recycled more easily — not only due to PR but because they benefit from it. After a while, you will see more players, in particular the bigger ones, joining the system and then there is something like a public buzz about it. And then there is no reason for the neighboring cities not to join in, and with it, the system gains momentum and scale.

Important to remember is: This systemic change requires significant preparation up front — you need to start with a theory of case, followed by a theory of change, and then a theory of catalyst. Are we there yet? Not quite. But we can see patterns emerging, and we can feel an upward spiral that moves faster and faster.

What kind of skills does systemic change require?

I think some of it is intellectual, and some of it is personality and mindset.

On the intellectual level, we need to learn to scope the problem properly. In analysis for systemic change, there are so many more things to get wrong than to get right. It's difficult to get the scope right when you are not changing a product or optimizing a single company's performance, but trying to build an entire new system in which the subject of analysis is an entire value chain.

Questions revolve around: What are the boundaries of our current system? What actually is our system? What does the system we envision look like?

Typically, you find out very soon when you don't get the question right — because your scope will be too narrow to deliver meaningful impact, even when you reach an answer to your question. And you also know that the scope might be too large when the answer is too complex to be implemented. One criterion to assess the quality of the scope of my question is to see if I have tried to capture all potential sources of value in the value chain.

How do you raise a generation of systemic change leaders?

For me, collaboration is key, and collaboration is a team sport. I find it very tragic that we are forcing our younger generations (and that includes my children who are still in school) into a race they will so easily lose against the machine. So we need to strengthen skills that are not made redundant by AI; and it's important to start early in the education process.

We need a system that equips us with skills and knowledge and that encourages experiences and goes beyond training of the intellect or the left brain, as Ken Robinson would say. Schools should be places that reward experimentation, collaboration, and risk-taking, so that we can all experience the change we want to be. In today's world, where things move so fast, you really need to keep a positive and open mind to think and see the change that you think is meaningful to our world.

Currently, in school, we teach all subjects separately. We have a math class, followed by an hour of English, then one of sports. In a complex, multi-parameter world, we need to be creative in bringing topics together that work together. I'm sure there is a way to combine geography and English. Some schools already do that, and we need more of this multidisciplinarity and playfulness in the children's curricula. Why don't we have a topic like "history of science"? And if you want to be super creative, you can ask the children to write their own poems to memorize facts. We can leverage many more integrated and natural ways of learning. I think math is quite danceable. It's probably easier said than done, and it requires understanding that humans are more than just their intellect! If we don't believe it's possible, we will never start acting on it!

In our company, we foster five traits as professional guidelines: creativity, challenge, change, care, and collaboration. We look at them when we bring new people on board. When we give each other feedback, we also speak about how we relate and live these values. Going for the five Cs is one way to avoid rigidity in thinking. In my view, none of them are easily substituted by artificial intelligence.

What else would you like to share with us?

What might have been bearable for the world in the past is now reaching an order of magnitude that calls for us to reconsider our economic system. If we believe the problem discussed earlier is not entirely untrue, we need to build strong societies that have functioning governance systems in place and that take action through societal discourse. Since systems are made of humans, I think the real revolution must start inside each of us.

First, we have to make sure that we don't waste a single minute of our lives on things that don't matter to us or that don't contribute to the change we want to see. So find yourself an assignment, a job, or build your own company where you can live in harmony with this bigger picture. Let's not spend time from Monday to Friday on anything that does not pay toward something meaningful. And by the way, I think this does not need to be at odds with ambitions, career progression, or even economic rewards, because in the end, when you have the balls to do what you care about, chances are you will do it very well! In my view, we should ask ourselves: "Am I a contributor to the well-being of my community?" In this way, we can safeguard the interest of society. If you ask people, "what really makes you happy?" the answers they give typically evolve around connectedness and identity. We need to understand that real prosperity, happiness, and fulfillment are linked to our own contribution.

Second, we need to make sure that we manage our energy well so that we can still enjoy our lives along the way. Contributing needs to go hand in hand with joy. We need fun and playfulness in our lives to generate the energy needed to keep up our motivation, think big, and to inspire others. Only when we're at ease with ourselves can we be good change leaders. And we can't afford not to be good leaders.

For me, the pillars of a balanced life are my family, nature, and the enormously satisfying feeling that we live in a world where there are no ceilings to possibility on Earth if we just start to live in an open-minded way. My family is big, and it provides me with a sense of responsibility, but it's also like my personal power plant I can tap into that generates a lot of energy for me.

I'm a geologist by training, and I have always loved to be in nature. In Laudato si', Pope Francis essentially said we got it wrong, religiously and philosophically. We have believed having a contract between individuals and society, and one between individuals and the spirit is sufficient. He says we also need a contract between the individual and nature. In my opinion, we have been forgetful of that; we need to urgently revisit our contract with our planet. If we acknowledge our responsibility, we can also bring a sense of rewarding fulfillment and energy back into our lives. And finally, there is this mind-blowing and, to me, almost addictive sense of possibility. Let's drop this narrative that we live in a narrow world because it's just not true. Life's too short for that. Let's stop feeling bad about what we do for a living. Feel free to readjust in case you find out that you got it wrong. I've gotten many things wrong in my life — but that's just how it goes when you work on things that potentially change systems.

Wouldn't it be wonderful if the largest and oldest democracies actually had the skills and the guts to demonstrate that they're prepared for a positive future and that they can address today's challenges in a way that is equitable, sustainable, and democratic? In this way, we wouldn't need to rely on autocratic regimes to steer us through transformation. This is the most challenging test we face as humankind, as the aggregate of individuals. It's the problem statement for my everyday work, in my roles as university professor, founding partner of a management consultancy, husband and father of six, and as a farmer.

I hope that in five years, we will be able to say that democracy has passed the test. We were ready to transform ourselves, and we did not give up when it seemed impossible to navigate the world of chaos because we had our own long-term vision, and we stood together, as Europeans and as humankind.

Beautiful brains change tomorrow...today
Brain-brush reflection exercise:

How did I feel when I read this?

What did I learn?

What will I integrate into my daily life?

In nature lies the answer to climate change

Luca Urbano,
founder at Food From Forest

What topic is currently most relevant for you?

Nowadays, we don't really see where food or any materials we use in our daily life come from. When you look at this cup of coffee that we are drinking — we don't really know where it comes from. So my work for now, and I have to admit it's a little bit of an obsession, is to find ways to help human beings rediscover their relationship with nature. I dedicate a lot of my time to understanding and working with food forestation, forest gardening or in French *forêt-jardin*. It's an ancestral way of growing food through planting trees. In my work, I can experience first hand how forests contribute to maintaining biodiversity of our ecosystem by being home to animals and wild plants.

If we look at forests holistically, we can see that there are so many more benefits that the forest can bring to the farmer than the farmer can bring to the forest. A food forest is of much more value to a farmer than seasoned crops, such as a field of rice, wheat, or corn. The problem with these crops is that they only last for a season, something like six months, and then, when you harvest them, you have only bare land left, and you have to plant again. In food forestation, farmers grow perennial crops, crops that last for several periods — for instance, some plants will be planted for three years, and others could live for hundreds of years. When you're a food forest farmer, you know very well how much your existence depends on the forest — it's important for your survival to keep the forest healthy. In essence, it's a way of farming that has a strong emphasis on respect toward the natural environment and aims at creating a bond between the human being and nature. I spend most of my time thinking about social and business strategies to bring to life this vision of a healthy, nourishing, and sustainable food forest system. This is the more philosophical aspect of my answer. From an environmental aspect, I'm obsessed with food forestation because it can provide a solution to climate change; one that we call the natural solution to climate change. Trees and plants have developed over billions of years the capability to absorb carbon from our atmosphere and fix it into our soil. There are ways of farming that are more efficient for sequestering carbon and storing it in the soil and that release less carbon into the atmosphere. Food forestation is only one technique, there are many more, such as permaculture or zero-tillage farming, that are also applicable to season crop farming. When you till the soil, you break it, and when the soil is broken, it releases carbon, which bonds with O_2, to create CO_2. No-tillage farming is a low-carbon technique in a way that you try not to break the soil and as such reduce emissions while preserving soil life. All these techniques are not only beautiful in their capacity to provide an intellectual answer to climate change, but they are also scalable techniques to bring food to the table. Scientific research proves that we could become carbon neutral by increasing soil carbon by only 0.4 percent per year, absorbing all global annual emissions. Obviously, we will still need to sequester the excess CO_2 that we have amassed in the atmosphere over the course of industrialization. So even from a macro-level perspective, food forestation makes a lot of sense; and there are plenty of social benefits it can bring to our social systems. The idea is to create a system that needs very little labor input. One of the thought leaders in sustainability is Gunter Pauli, the author of the book *Blue Economy.* He studies the efficiency of natural systems in very interesting ways. In the current agriculture system, you put one calorie of energy (mostly based on oil), and you get two to three calories out of that. It's not very efficient. Farmers in South America that engage in agro-ecology methods have a ratio of one to twenty. So there are already methods in the market that have proven more efficient than our large-scale agriculture!

What is the social aspect of food-forestation?

In general, it's not only about farming techniques, the benefits are much more all-encompassing. One of the biggest drivers of carbon emissions is transportation. When we create local food systems, we contribute to reduction of these emissions. What I love about food foresting is that the forest does not only provide food, it provides wood, honey, shelter, and so on — many things that we humans need to survive and create income. Food foresting is a technique that has been used by communities in South America and Africa, right after they stopped hunting and gathering. It requires the use of our hands. There is little room for standardization, It's not a technique that can be done by machines. It's a technique that caters best to small-scale farmers. We know from data from the UN Food and Agriculture Organization, that around eighty percent of consumed food in our world is produced by small-scale farmers. These are farmers that have less than one hectare or 10,000 square meters of land; and they farm their land mostly by hand, or with very little support from technology. From a community perspective, it is also a sustainable way to integrate old people into the value creation process. They can only work two to three hours a day, and they cannot engage in heavy physical labor. In a food forest, they only need to pick some fruits.

When we think about agriculture, in my view, working with forests is the most appropriate way for many reasons. Food forests require a little bit of time in the beginning, but over the years, they are self-sustaining sources of food and revenues. It's a very diverse system. There is no defined way to do that. Everybody is still experimenting with different forest designs, plants, different trees. The design of the forest also varies between climates. There is no one book to follow. Our vision is that every time we bring people together and share their learnings from their own forests, we can spark this exchange of knowledge and help the entire community to co-create their own community way of food foresting.

With food foresting, we also create a platform for people to come together and talk about topics they all have in common. The discussions revolve around discoveries. Others would be inspired to try the same design as well. We don't know yet where the discussions will lead, but we are now trying to select and develop some standardized exchange tools for participants. We make use of games and creative interventions like creating maps on soil so that we can all exchange information in an informal way that is not "written" in stone. We also have local committees that are responsible for finding ways to document the outcomes of the sessions in a way that can be accessible by other communities or members that were not present and that also show the evolution of the knowledge within the community.

In my food-forestation work, we plant moringa trees. The locals call moringa a miracle tree because it has very thick, balloon-shaped roots that soak and save water. This makes it very resilient to dryness — it can survive up to six months without water! You can use all of its different parts for production. The tree provides an abundance of nutrients in times where there is not much to gain and in a place where many people suffer from malnutrition. The leaves can be harvested and dried; they are the queen of superfoods because they are highly nutritious. They contain plenty of vitamins such as A, B, C, and E, and they are rich in minerals like calcium and iron, antioxidants, and up to twenty-five percent of the plant consists of proteins. On top of that, it is a very fast growing tree. Within the food forestation ecosystem, it's one of the pioneering plants; it's the plant that you plant first to get your food forest started. In general, food forestation is more of a long term investment — in tropical climates it takes about two to five years until you have reached a good level of production to generate stable income. But with moringa, already three months after planting the seeds, you can harvest the first leaves to make moringa powder. And after around eighteen months, the moringa plant can also give you seeds, which are also edible or from which you can produce oil. In a forest, there is biodiversity, there are multiple layers of plants that can provide shadows to each other and that can pass on nutrients to each other, either via their root systems or via wildlife and birds. The most common current solutions to malnutrition is to supply people food. It helps in the short term — but is not sustainable. Growing food locally is actually not common practice, even not in areas that are suffering from malnutrition. One of the main problems in local farming is access to water. A lot of time is spent on collecting water, whether it's for drinking or for agriculture. Even when Congo has vast freshwater resources, there are very few irrigation systems available. So most of the farmers who don't live close to a river or a lake cannot really grow anything outside of the rainy season. And in Congo, there are six months of dry season in the year. This is where food forestation and moringa come in.

Where did you find your passion for ancient farming techniques?

Well, it's almost like a miracle, and I'd almost say I was very lucky, even when I don't really believe in the concept of luck. I'll share with you my life hack: When you break an object, it releases energy. If you can channel this energy, it can create a new and beautiful structure. That's how the evolution of humans in general or how the Industrial Revolution happened, right? Throughout history, we have broken structures, and thereby we have released energy that was then used to create new structures. And in these moments of disorder and chaos, we have moments where we can actually shape new structures. These are really powerful moments to shape history. We should use this power wisely, it's the best we can do. And we should do it in a balanced way. Too much passion can have adverse effects because in your rush, there is a risk that you stop listening to others and that you lose the ability to calmly observe the facts. When this happens, you may end up stuck in a dead end. One of the most important life lessons I had to learn — and it took me quite a while to understand this — is that there are some things that you just can't do alone. I had grown up wanting and in fact doing everything by myself in order to protect my own ideas; and I guess I was scared of letting go of my ideas. During my childhood, I spent a few years in Kinshasa with my family. My father worked for the Italian corporation agency. I had many passions and no passions, so I ended up skipping classes and so on. I was quite a free mind and some sort of a rebel. I looked everywhere outside of school to find some kind of orientation and at the same time, I didn't want to commit to any one thing at all. Sometime during university, I felt this strong urge to understand more of life. I wanted to understand who I was, and I was looking for a purpose or meaning I was craving to learn, just learn I spent plenty of time by myself, researching about anything that caught my interest and trying to find the theme in my life.

I studied business, but actually I spent so much more time figuring out what life is about, just letting my thoughts guide me to wherever they wanted to. I like to compare it to dancing. I love dancing, and when I dance, it makes me feel like I'm in flow, I'm all by myself. I don't need to follow any steps, like in classical dance, but I can just move my body freely. To me, this is expression of life, to react spontaneously to what the rhythm and the music suggest. While I dance, I become more aware of the movements of my body, of the thoughts in my head, of the way I react to the moment. My thoughts slow down, there is silence in my head, and I can see clearly what is happening inside me and around me. And because of this, I can be in flow with the music and I become a very creative person. I create my own dance. I move quicker, and yet, time slows down for me, maybe because I am more aware of what I'm doing. It's like broadening the angle of my perspective from sixty degrees to 180 degrees. So when I get stuck, I just bring my body into movement and settle into the natural rhythm of life. In general, I think when you get stuck, just stop whatever you're doing and at least go for a little walk. When you move, that's when you break habits, that's when you move into a new rhythm. But there is one caveat to this way of learning:

It has limitations if you pursue it by yourself. There is some secret sauce to expanding your growth, and I'd say it is linked to the power of sharing. Only when I met my wife Chiara, and we went to East Congo together to found a not-for-profit organization, Mazao, I discovered how powerful it is when you can do something in trustful co-creation.

When you share your ideas with another person, then you open a space for this person to enrich your idea with their own perspective. Chiara added so many flavors to our project that would have never crossed my mind. And sometimes, she just helps me to see things that I wouldn't be able to see alone. There was a moment when I tried to make a decision about the supply chain for our project. In one of our project regions, Tanganjika, in the East of DR Congo, close to a city called Kalemie, around ninety-five percent of rice is imported. We wanted to buy local rice, to support the local economy. Local farmers were very happy with this, and they started to grow more rice. We had entered into a battle with rice importers. But very soon, there was not enough rice in the local market to meet our demand for production, so we had to get on a train and travel all over the country finding different sources of local rice. From a cost perspective, it didn't make a lot of sense. Nevertheless, I still believed, it was worth all the hustle, just to prove a point, and I didn't listen to my wife Chiara, who was pushing for leaving this ideological battle and just making sure that we could meet our production capacity. In hindsight, it was a battle against the laws of physics — a battle that we would have never been able to win, in particular because it was slowly eating into our cash flow. Still, I kept pushing for it. I was so sure that we would find a sustainable solution. The solution never came, and then we crashed. That's when I learned the hard way that there is something such as too much motivation or too much passion. Sometimes, when you have so much of your heart dedicated toward one specific object or idea, you will go all the extra miles that it takes to achieve this one idea. It feels very great to go all in. You want more and more. That's very dangerous, and you need to be careful. Don't confuse addiction with flow! You actually need to be able to pass the ball back and forth to keep the game flowing by reacting to whatever challenges come up in a humble and nimble way. It was amazing, because it felt like for the first time in my life I was seeing some kind of bigger picture. This is when life turns into flow.

What do we need to know about working in Congo?

East Congo is a very blessed region. It is abundant in fertile land and plenty of fresh water. However, it is also a region that has been in a challenging political situation for a long period; there have been so many conflicts. The local communities, with whom we work, have been attacked many times. As a consequence, the local communities move a lot, and every time they move, we have to restart our project. One of the biggest challenges we faced was to build resilience in a very fragile environment. In Congo, there are around 300 tribes who all have their own languages, rituals, arts, religion, and so on. One driver of unity and of division in Congo is tribalism. The main ethnic group is called Bantu; and the word means people. Mutu is one person, and Bantu are two and more people. In Congo, it's quite common that you follow some modern religion such as Christianity or Islam and that you are an animist or follow something like a Bantu cosmology at the same time. It would not be an atypical situation where the leader of a tribe is a Muslim, his or her right hand is a Christian, and the left hand is an atheist. In their system, hierarchy and equality go hand in hand. So there are clear rules of who is in decision-making power within the community. They used to be mainly hunters and gatherers, and some of them practice food forestation.

When I was in Kalemie, I would sometimes meet up with an old Congolese Bantu Catholic priest, to learn about Bantu philosophy. There is a lot of respect towards all community members. Communities are set up in a way that they are dependent on each other for survival. One day, you might not have found food, but your neighbor might have. Sharing and collaboration is key for the survival of the community, and in order to keep this function alive, they place a lot of energy and focus on building relationships. They also worship their ancestors quite a lot. It doesn't end with interpersonal relationships. They also have these very strong bonds with nature. They praise their ancestors and nature because they think we are indivisible from them. We can only be who and where we are today because of them. They consider nature a living spirit, and they even have different spirits for different parts of nature. There is this invaluable treasure of knowledge about the medical benefits of local plants. You may think that this is somewhat of a naive or romantic rural tradition, but I have found that even in the cities where most people are Christians and somehow considered more educated and rational, this strong bond with nature and ancestors plays an important role in their everyday lives.

Due to the history of war in Congo, people are focused on the short term. They don't know if there will be another conflict tomorrow, so thinking ahead of the next season is not too important to them. They are a little bit scared to invest into things that might not work out. Having a step-by-step model helps. It provides security because you can already harvest some fruits early, and you will always have food available — even when you're sick and you cannot come and work in your garden too much. In terms of business operations, one of the key learnings was that it is very important to source locally when you are in these kinds of dynamic environments. In the beginning, we imported many things, but then, whenever things broke down, we had a bottleneck in our supply chain. So we had to think about ways to be locally self-sustaining. Further, one of the challenges when we start anew is the mindset of our clients. They have been trained by decades of western development aid to be paid for attending any kind of participatory sessions. Locals are used to getting paid for being trained. We invest a lot of time into demonstrating the benefits of the food forest system and building a commercial relationship with local farmers. We buy their leaves at a given price, and we offer them consultation to make best use of their land.

What is important to us is that farmers get to do their own landscape design and are making their own decisions as to which planting strategies they want to follow. Asking local farmers to create their own maps in the soil using leaves and some branches is an important starting point. Nobody knows about the qualities of his land better than the farmer himself. He knows about the slope, the distance to the river, the history of the land. He owns the knowledge, and we help him or her create the scenario that suits their individual situation best. Our job is to facilitate the thinking process. We help them understand what kind of opportunities there are to increase resilience of their forest system or what kind of investments they need to make to cultivate their forest.

What do you want to share with the world?

This summer, I was with my little daughter in a building. We wanted to go downstairs, and I thought she had gone with my wife, so I took the stairs. At one point in time, I heard her crying very loudly and forcefully. It turned out that my wife Chiara had thought she was with me. I ran up the stairs to the seventh floor, hugged her, and she stopped crying. That moment made me realize that this little girl probably had for the first time in her life felt a fear that she had never felt before. Fear is very powerful in that it pushes our boundaries. She had constructed that reality in her mind, that if she cried, we would come and help her. I believe she grew from this experience. Fear can be helpful, to leap forward and empower ourselves to take action because we create structures when we feel fear. The only thing I know for sure is that we humans have this infinite capacity to experience freedom, creativity, and hope. It's infinite because even if we lose everything else, we will not lose this freedom until we die. We were given this gift by evolution. We can lose a lot of things related to our existence in one day, like our projects, our mission, and so on. The only obstacle we have to make full use of this infinite, is fear. The only way I have found to be able to break free from this fear, is to break free from rigid structures. Fear and creativity, they are interlinked. We can use it as an opportunity to push ourselves forward towards this idea of hope and freedom.

Beautiful brains change tomorrow...today
Brain-brush reflection exercise:

How did I feel when I read this?

What did I learn?

What will I integrate into my daily life?

We need mindfulness and kindness to thrive in complex systems

Dr. Ralf Schneider, group CIO of Allianz SE

What topic is currently most relevant for you?

We live in a world that is more connected than ever in human history, and this interconnectedness is growing exponentially. Thanks to the internet, we are now able to access humankind's pooled knowledge from all over the globe and at any time. We use social media to network with each other, and we have also started to connect machines with machines, and machines with humans. The results are that we are now part of global hyper-dynamic networks. My topic of interest is: "How can humanity cope with the ever-increasing complexity and perhaps even benefit from it?"

When I think of complexity in organizations, I think of Ashby's law of requisite variety, that, in a simplified way, says that "only variety absorbs variety." It's a concept from cybernetics, the science of communications and control systems. It says that in order for a system to be stable, it needs to at least mirror the magnitude of disorders of the outside world. Organizations need to connect inside themselves, but also need to connect outside of their organizational boundaries to master the complexity caused by the disorders of the outside world. It's the quality and quantity of intra- and interpersonal connections, that help to keep an organization stable in times of rapid change and system inherent interconnectedness through technology and globalization.

Let's look at a simplified network model with ten people, in which every person is connected with each other bidirectionally, and in which a person (that is, a knot in the network) can only have two states: it works or it does not work. How many states can this network have? The simplified answer is: two to the power of (ten times nine) states. That is two to the power of 90, which is a number so large that our human brain just cannot really grasp it. In comparison, the universe has two to the power of 78 atoms. The company I work with, Allianz, we have more than 140,000 employees. Now just imagine a world of seven billion people, or a universe full of stars and the sheer infinite amount of possible states there can be. How would we be able to find the one optimal "state" of the world? There is a very complex problem, no machine, no human being can solve. Complex problems are ones where you have to make assumptions about situations that are uncertain, and where the underlying information set is incomplete and will always stay incomplete. It is a problem where the interaction is highly dynamic to the extent that it goes beyond our possibilities to calculate it. One of the most complex systems is the human being. It is impossible to fully rationally understand us. We have more than ninety billion neurons in our brains and you can just imagine how impossible it is to really understand what pathways between these neurons could look like. In complex systems, we cannot rationalize.

How do we deal with complexity?

I have observed three types of strategies. The ones that just deny complexity in the systems and treat problems as if they were linear. Then there are a set of strategies that do trial and error. And the third type of strategy is dominated by trying to rationally understand and build models that are more and more complicated. In our culture, we are mostly following the third strategy. We try to understand complex problems rationally — but the fact is that in highly complex systems, rationality has its boundaries. When you try to solve complex problems intellectually only, what you come up with is only a partial solution. What I think is more necessary than ever is to also follow our intuition. Intuition, to me, is a decision-making skill that develops as a result of recurring exposure to a set of similar conditions. It goes beyond just thinking about a problem; it's ingrained in your different senses. This happens when you have been exposed to the same problem a few times and you have developed expertise in analyzing the common features of the problem, understood the underlying pattern, and automated the process to cope with these problems. When you face challenging situations that require you to find a different way of re-action, you will develop intuition. Because it requires you to move outside of your autopilot reaction. Intuition is expertise, but it goes beyond intellectual expertise in that it involves emotional expertise as well.

Let's get back to our complex world. In a complex world, things change very fast. Our day has twenty-four hours. It's impossible to learn everything by yourself. So the way I learn to develop my own intuition is to connect with others, as many as possible, who have been exposed to different environments than I have. Most likely, they have developed a very different intuition, and so I can learn from them. Their skillset enriches mine. When you connect with people who have a very different view and a different mechanism of pattern analysis, you expand your own expertise. We learn, and we grow, and that is due to complexity that asks us to connect and collaborate with others. When we do that a few times, repeatedly, it's something I call the interpersonal explosion of consciousness. Complexity drives progress for humankind. It's a circle. And when we know how to connect and learn with each other, we do not need to fear our world of seven billion people. We do not need to fear conflicts, refugee influx, a growing gap between rich and poor.

In this kind of dynamic network, we need three types of people. The creatives, that is the ones that envision new ideas and solutions. They can be a little bit annoying sometimes because they develop plenty of ideas. I'm sometimes a little bit too creative, and that brings instability to the system as well. Then, you need the topic owners. These are people, that have the inherent motivation to become thought leaders in a certain field, let's say quantum computing. You can't develop new relevant solutions without experts. And finally, you have the network brokers. They are the ones who connect the creatives with the experts. What all of them need in order to connect in a relevant way, is a minimum level of mindful communication skills.

How do we build the skill of interpersonal connection?

I think the basic requirement is intrapersonal awareness. I need to understand myself, in order to understand others. It's not a linear process though — by talking to others, and observing what happens inside me while I interact with them, I also learn a lot about myself. This is, oddly, how I got to understand myself. But interpersonal connection is also just by going online. With the internet nowadays, you can just connect with people all around the world. Mindfulness is a great way to make meaningful connections. For me, what works best is to go into a conversation and try to understand the other person as much as possible.

The biggest obstacle for connection, in my point of view, is that we tend to put a value label to every human interaction. We also value ourselves — many people think that they are only worth something when they perform to some standards. Attaching identity to some value is very dangerous. We need to understand that A and non-A are equally-valid. That we as humans, that we are all equally-valid.

What is the purpose of a human life, if we don't have a value to live for?

I'd love to refer to Professor Markus Gabriel, who says, "There is no answer to the question: What is the meaning of life! There is only an answer to the question: What is the meaning of my own life?" And the quest for your own life purpose is an exciting journey to embark on. However, in my belief, there are human values, that apply to all different cultures, called universal values. You can synthesize them in the golden rule, which says: "Do unto others as you would have others do unto you." If every human being followed this rule, we wouldn't be able to have built or continue to build the systems we are currently living in. And what is really sad is that we are spending so much of our energies into convincing each other that this rule is not valid. We try to convince ourselves that consumption leads to happiness; or, like the Chinese are currently doing it, that enforced conformity of thoughts is the key to happiness. A lot of people think that we have to do something in order to be happy. It's actually not true. Most of the time, we don't have to do anything. We are actually entitled to do something!

So to bring this back to the organizational level, I think there are three mindsets or values that are helpful to build interpersonal connection in an interaction between human beings: Curiosity, the skill to ask relevant questions, mindfulness, and kindness. Curiosity means, that you train yourself to be open minded and generous towards the other person. You need to really want to understand the other person! Asking the right question implies that you listen carefully. Typically, in communication, we convey signals between two people. It's a transfer of signals that contain information. In order to make this process of signal transfer most efficient, I need to understand myself very well. Else, there is a lot of noise in my communication and my signal is confusing. And it's very difficult to ask a relevant question, when I don't even know how to interpret my own signals! One of my favorite writers, the Austrian Stefan Zweig, says: "One who has understood the human inside himself, understands all humans." Understanding humans is also about understand how this human was brought up, what kind of challenges they have lived through in their lives, how they have coped with these challenges? You can learn a lot from and about another person when you understand their biggest crises in life. This helps me understand why he or she says or sees something the way they say or see it. When you have understood the social context of the other person, it's not that difficult to understand their technical view on some problems. And this can take you very far in the business world as well. It's not only about opening up emotionally. It's about getting to the core of a problem. In this case it was the core of interpersonal relationships. And mindfulness is about this intrapersonal skill I mentioned earlier. I need to understand what is happening inside me while I'm engaging in an activity with another human being. And kindness is, in my experience, the best conduit within human interaction.

In the business context, it's about getting to the core of a real problem, a technical problem. Only if we get to the core of a problem instead of dancing around it, can we solve it. And let's face it, in today's complex world, nobody is able to solve their problems alone anymore, so we also need to understand that we need to connect, collaborate, and open up. It's very simple: when you open up, you realize that actually everybody carries some kind of emotional dirtbag and then we don't really need to hide anything anymore. It requires also a mindset of humbleness. There are people who can do all three things at the same time. I think I'm quite good in wanting to understand people, and throughout my career, I also have learned to ask the right questions. What I'm really working on is being mindful with myself — what's happening inside me while I'm engaging in an interaction. I have to admit that I'm still a rookie when it comes to mindfulness in interactions… it's only by the end of 2018 that I really started to look into the practice of mindfulness.

How do you practice mindfulness?

The good thing about this mindfulness practice is that I can practice it in every interaction. The way I learn new things is to focus on a few things that I find most relevant and then develop catch phrases that I try to integrate into my daily life. In a conversation with someone about mindfulness, we spoke about different dimensions of mindfulness. Well, I picked two of them, just to start off with. One is that everything is equally-valid. So when I encounter uncomfortable emotions, such as impatience or anger, I try to just observe them and see what they try to communicate to me. I have come to understand that emotions are just signals that bear important information, so I don't deny them or suppress them. For example, what is my anger telling me about me? It helps that I'm a curious person by nature, so now, when I feel that I get angry, I try to smile at my anger and explore what is behind it. There is some upside to being an impatient person: I have never had a problem making a timely executive decision. The second thing I try to practice is looking at another person as a blank sheet of paper, even when I seemingly know the other person very well. It's a fun way of entering into an interaction when you just look at the other person with a fresh mind and try to listen to the subtle nuances in their communication. It's fascinating, there is so much to discover even with people with whom you have worked for years! You just reach a new level of quality in your conversations, in your interactions, when you try to understand each other and tune into it.

How do you have mindful conversations in the workplace?

I think it's easiest to start with yourself. In general, I think there is at least one person with whom you need to meet with unconditional kindness: yourself. There is no reason not to do so. If this is not possible for you, then you know where to start with personal development work. Then practice in bilateral interactions. And then practice in small groups. I'm convinced that mindful conversation can only happen with groups no more than eight to ten people. So team meetings that are larger don't really work when you want to practice mindfulness. Keep it small. For larger groups, there are more effective tools, such as Professor Fredmund Malik's Syntegration approach. I implemented the principles of mindfulness as a mindset in my last strategic team offsite. Every team member presented, and we did not interrupt them. Then, for the feedback, it was the same. Pure feedback. No interruption. And no need for justification. I think, it was the best offsite I've had for a while. We listened to each other genuinely, and with the intention to support each other becoming the team player we want to become. This helps to set a strong foundation to solving problems at the workplace efficiently and sustainably.

Have you always been your own best friend?

I'm not 100% sure, but I believe so. I have always had the other problem, in that I may not have been critical with myself. It's not like I'm not disciplined or don't work hard… it's maybe that I might have focused a little bit too much towards solving technical problems to the detriment of the emotional side. I was very impatient when something didn't work out or somebody didn't deliver. Some people would say I had a choleric tendency. It has happened that people have started to cry in my meetings. I never did this on purpose; it just happened. My father had these choleric tendencies as well, and for me, this was never really something that bothered me. In my friend's circle, family circle, people didn't really bother my temper either. But in a professional setting, a similar behavior has a different impact. Instilling fear in your co-workers is not really helpful in solving problems because people who are scared just block. It happens very fast. And then you never get to solve the problem. Unfortunately, it took me quite a long time to come to this realization. In 2012, I had a profound life trigger event when my father unexpectedly passed away during a hike. It was not an accident or so, he just suffered from a stroke. And I asked myself: "What is the sense of my life? This can't be it?" I realized that I'm a very fortunate person in my role as a corporate leader. I can make a lot of people very happy because I can help them develop their human potential. This is applicable to each person. But if you are in a leadership position, your options are just manifold!

What I have always loved to do is motivate others to become their best version. When people reach their goals, I also feel very excited, it means a lot to me to see my employees grow. Sometimes, I have not been very mindful with this capacity. When you motivate people too much, you may burn them out. It also took quite some time, until I was able to put my learnings into practice. Of course you still have to deliver on your goals in an organization like ours — else you will not be able to keep this privilege of being a leader in this system. There is a lot of pressure in big corporations. As a leader, it is very important that you can stand against this pressure. So many leaders just forward the pressure to their employees, which is not a great leadership quality, I find. I learned it a little bit late, and at the same time, it's very difficult to say if a different approach would have led me to the C-Level position I am today. Organizations are complex systems, there is no black or white.

The problem I see is, that in our current systems, followers don't really want to step up! Decision-making causes fear for responsibility. Even when I tell you: "I will take the responsibility for whatever happens, I'll take full responsibility for any blame." Reality shows that this is difficult to convey in a way employees will believe it. They need to experience it! It takes a lot of time to build this trust, to build this safe environment. Whenever I get new employees, the same game starts anew.

What do you want to share with the world?

I feel I want to put an emphasis on these three things: be curious, be kind, be mindful with any interactions and you will experience flashes of magic so powerful you can't even imagine. The magic is in the creativity and co-creation that unfolds when you dive into collaboration with others from an open mindset. In essence, I would love to interact with my colleagues the same way as with my friends. I'm not a big fan of separating business and private life. It's impossible because we are one person.

Our current system is not really built for these authentic connections yet, but I'm working everyday with my team to co-create this safe workplace where we can all be authentic, trust in each other, and become mindful leaders. We've still got a long way to go, but I think we are on a good path. It's a never-ending journey of becoming. Becoming the person we want to be, and being able to contribute in the way we find meaningful into a system that is ever-changing. Sometimes, in network organizations, you are the influencer or the leader, and sometimes you are the follower. It would be a dream to just switch between being a leader and follower. I don't want to be a guru, I love to learn and be led by others as well. I'm not sure how this can be implemented. Ideally, we can just switch on and off, we'd have skills to move swiftly between these roles when we communicate clearly who is in what role. The Holocaust survivor and psychiatrist Viktor Frankl said that freedom is in the moment between stimulus and response. For me, this is a very profound teaching. The way it relates to me is that we have freedom in our ability to respond to a certain trigger. Our responsibility as a leader is in fine tuning our response-ability.

Yip's note: The quote from Viktor Frankl is originally from Stephen Covey, thanks to information from Alexander Vesely, Frankl's grandson.

Beautiful brains change tomorrow...today
Brain-brush reflection exercise:

How did I feel when I read this?

What did I learn?

What will I integrate into my daily life?

Holistic decision-making in interconnected social systems

Xiaowei Rose Luo,
associate professor of Entrepreneurship and Family Enterprise at INSEAD

What is the topic that fascinates you most?

I grew up in China, and in our culture, we are trained to look at the impact of our individual actions on the collective. It's not okay in this environment to only act in your best interest, but I need to see how my behavior will influence my family, my school, and so on. Even if I wanted to pursue self interest, I'd need to frame it in a way that is acceptable to the collective. It is natural for me to analyze things from a systems' perspective. So I became a doctoral student in the field of sociology. In this field, we try to understand in which way the structure and the context in which we live can shape the way we think and make decisions. Now I am a business professor and I live in France, working with international business students and executives.

People who grew up in Western societies have focused more on reflecting about individual decision-making, which also has its strengths. My fascination is to look at how we can combine different perspectives rooted in our cultural backgrounds to understand systems in a more holistic way. When we bring all of these different perspectives and reflect about them together, we have an enriched source of information for decision making. It's important to me to produce high quality research that is not only meeting rigorous scientific standards in terms of design and data gathering. It's also important to me that managers find the conclusions from my work relevant and useful for their work.

In a globalized world, our societies have turned into complex dynamic systems. This requires the capability to sometimes let go of our views that we hold tightly. It's not always helpful to be judgmental — discussing which system is better than another system is only fruitful if you understand both systems very well. I'm trying to find ways to help managers understand the relationship between the business world and society.

What would be differences between the Eastern and Western cultural context?

In the Western cultural context, when you do something, you expect other people to pay you a reward that is linked to this specific thing or action. In the Eastern cultural context, it's a little bit more indirect. I should give you a specific example to illustrate this: I have a student who did an internship in China. After the internship, she received a request from her former colleague to do some market research. She gladly agreed, and after delivery, she waited for the payment. A few weeks passed, nothing happened. She contacted the former colleague, and hinted indirectly at the outstanding payment, but still, nothing happened. Finally, she couldn't hold herself back anymore, and she asked directly for her reward. The former colleague felt really hurt. She said: "How could you expect me to pay for this work? I was expecting you to do me a favor." My student was very shocked by this reaction, and she got very upset as well. To her, it seemed unfair because she had put in all the work and expected to be directly rewarded for it. In the Eastern context, even when people expect you to do this as a favor, it doesn't mean they're ungrateful people. They will be looking for another opportunity to return this favor to you.

As a result of misunderstandings like the above, many foreign people find it really uncomfortable to do business in China. They feel like it's a manipulative environment. They describe their business partner as dishonest, complicated, too much "under the table." People in China sometimes think of Western people as too utilitarian, too transactional, or too focused on the object rather than on the human being. But if you look at it more closely, it's just two different approaches to give and take. Each perspective actually has its advantages. The Western way of doing business can indeed improve efficiency and it might prevent some sources of misunderstanding because it takes vagueness out of the equation. And maybe it could be more ethical in some situations. I do think that we can all learn from each other. In cross-cultural management, it's therefore very important to understand the subtle differences and how contexts shape them.

I teach a field trip course called "Building business in China," where we visit local companies in China and speak with decision makers about topics such as innovation strategies. Many students have observations about Chinese companies, such as, "This company is just a copycat, not very interesting." It's a good starting point but we cannot stop there - we need to dive deeper into analyzing the context in which these companies operate. Indeed, many of the rapidly growing Chinese companies from the high tech sector started off as mere copycats before they then stepped up from pure imitation to local adaptation and then to something more unique. Some of them now are global leaders. The ones who do not manage this transition, typically fail in a very short time period. I want students to see with their own eyes what is happening on the ground so they can build their own view of the picture, rather than just relying on the sometimes very one-sided views provided by the media. One of the prevailing teaching methods in China is learning through imitation. So for Chinese students, copying is how they grow. It is not viewed as something negative. So from a societal perspective, imitation makes sense. If you look at it from an overall perspective, it is also a very natural development. It's not always smart to reinvent the wheel and start from scratch. Not only is it not very smart, but it's also not the best use of societal resources.

How do we set up businesses to operate in an environmentally sustainable way?

Corporate social responsibility is also one of my research areas that I really care about. Companies are not simply there to make a profit even though shareholders care a lot about it. I think, that in the long term, we as a society, cannot afford to have companies that are only interested in profits. It's simply unrealistic given the current trends of labor replacement, we also need to care about how we maintain a balance for people to find fulfillment. Let's take marketing strategy as an example. Of course, for companies to be sustainable, they have to find ways to inspire consumers to pay for their services. So as a company, it's very natural to want to optimize our marketing to gain a relevant share of the consumer wallet. A strong value system is one in which the individual decision makers in the company still debate the questions: How much is good enough? Where do we reach a threshold where the consumer will overspend? China, for example, has been criticized for a long time with regards to pollution. It's a fair claim — large scale manufacturing and this single-minded focus on GDP growth have resulted in environmental pollution. We do see these heavy polluting industries in many parts of the country, where air and water quality are very, very poor. At the same time, there are also a lot of good practices in China as well as in other developing countries. Many of these practices are very environmentally friendly and they are closely related to their own kind of economic disadvantages. Let me share an example: People in China are very thrifty. So many people re-use disposables such as plastic bags. Also for things in their homes such as glass jars and so on, they try to keep them and repurpose them. Whatever is left from their purchase, they find new ideas to use them over and over again. When they buy oil, they like to bring their own bottle, again, to save something. As a consumer goods company, for instance, you would design your product in a way that caters to the local market preferences anyway. Why not do it in a way that is both locally acceptable and also appealing to environmental sustainability?

How can companies enhance their intercultural management capabilities?

That's a big challenge. In international business we always talk about this tension, and the search for the one set of standard operating procedures, that we can then roll out across the globe. Many multinational players believe that optimizing our procedural efficiencies will also facilitate the management of the company. In my view, you have to look at different countries differently. In order for you to adapt successfully to a local market, you need to understand how people live their daily lives and then find ways to help them do it in a better way. The more different the local culture is from the headquarters, the more allowances or discretion you need to give them. Deviation is costly and can be time-consuming, but if you are too rigorous with your standard operation model, sometimes, you simply can't do the work.

When it comes to managing multinational teams, it's very important that people are trained about intercultural differences. As leaders, you need to create a safe and comfortable space for team members to learn how to speak their minds openly so that they can learn from each other's different opinions. Typically, you need trained facilitators or coaches to guide through these discussions. They need to train employees how to engage in open communication. It's necessary because without this professional training and a relationship based on mutual trust, employees may suffer from misunderstandings and hold grudges against each other and this will prevent them from having happy lives at work.

It seems that in China the government plays an important role. What are your recommendations to managers?

When it comes to working with the government, there are a lot of negative associations, right? For instance, many managers think they should be focused on investing their time on honing their core competencies, rather than spending time working with the government. However, when you move to a context where there is a lack of institutional and critical basic infrastructure, the government can play a very important role for the economy because it substitutes for this lack in infrastructure.

In China, for example, it is very important to spend time figuring out a good working relationship with the government. Governments are developmental, which means they are very willing to step in to fill these voids because they have clear growth objectives and are incentivized to help the local economy grow. The government has a very clear objective, and they want companies to contribute, so they are willing to move towards the companies. Government success is linked to very specific performance indicators such as growth rate of the economy, the amount of jobs provided. This measurement is broken down into the different levels of government, down to the local government. In general, government institutions see companies as partners that can help them reach their own goals.

There are certain industries that the Chinese national government would like to grow, and local governments will have high incentives to help you prosper. As a company, you need to find out if you can be positioned in these industries because that will put you in a position to benefit from local subsidies, tax rebates, and so on. You can see which provinces have an interest in attracting players like yours to join them. As a company, to thrive, you need to understand what is important to the government and then think about how you can align with the government on these objectives. In such a setting, government decision makers will sometimes go the extra mile to fulfill their own incentive systems. Companies should feel free to engage in this conversation so they can understand how to create opportunities for themselves and help meet the government objectives at the same time. In the Western world, we often see subsidies as something negative because it distorts the free market. In my view, we need to look a little bit deeper: From an ethical perspective, it's not a harmful action, if governments try to create win-win situations as long as it's done in a transparent way.

What is needed to increase awareness about ethical behavior in our current market systems?

Working with the government does not have to involve corruption and bribery. It is clear that as a company you shouldn't be using resources provided by the government to hurt society. It's just like encouraging individuals to do something they are passionate about and looking for people to sponsor them in their endeavors. Just don't get lost in the abundance of help offered — be clear about your original goals. And I think that's very, very important when you work with the government.

I emphasize this ethical point because once you have built a very strong and fruitful relationship with the government, that is, when you have helped them meet their objectives, you may receive many advantages from the government. In the end, government officials are also just human beings, and some of us human beings can be tempted to abuse our power during our careers, right? It takes a little bit of self-reflection to see when the advantages that are given by the governments might create an unfair competition; and in this area, the company needs to decide if it wants to restrain itself. That's also key to the long-term relationship between the company and the government, because once you get into the gray areas, you actually become more vulnerable, for example, for future retaliation. Recently, Tencent, a Chinese technology giant, who earns a big chunk of their business from online games, was penalized by the Chinese government for one of their major games due to unethical behavior, and their stock prices went down. Government retaliation is a serious risk, even very successful companies that may have invested considerably more time into thinking about corporate social responsibility can make mistakes.

In general, it is important for you to regularly revisit your purpose again: am I in this business simply to make as much profit as possible or do I really care about our employees and the community I operate in? When you create products, you need to make a strategic decision: Yes, as a corporation, we want our users to like our products and use them as often as possible, but do we want them to become addicted to these products?

There is a sociological reason why companies have focussed on maximizing financial value for their shareholders. Shareholder value maximization is a result of a history of individual decisions that have shaped the system in the way it is. In the traditional society, capital was not too important on the individual level because you needed high input of labor to produce a certain good. Nowadays, we have artificial intelligence and automation. With the rise of technology, labor as a production factor becomes less important over time, and capital is increasing in its importance. As a society, we have developed organizational knowhow to optimize efficiency in our companies, which means we have put ourselves in a situation where we use less labor. Capital has become a more important resource than labor, and it has become a scarce resource that we are competing for. That's why the people who are contributing the capital, the investors, feel entitled to demand a bigger return than a return that labor would yield. That's, very simply put, how shareholder maximization theory developed from a societal perspective. And within a system, that is built on competition mechanisms, that makes a lot of sense. It doesn't mean that this system is the most effective system for all times — but there is a reason why this system is the way it is right now. In general, decision-making is a socially constructed process.

I am not against technology, but I do not agree that capital should have the largest return. It's not in the best interest of society; it's not serving people's needs for fulfilling lives. We understand that people are happier when they are working because then they are a contributing member of society, they feel they can make other people happy. If we care about well-being, we cannot exclude labor from the value creation process, even when labor is not yielding high returns. If we as a society cannot provide jobs, we need to provide alternative means for people to live a fulfilled life. So this is where we can think about how we can leverage technology. Currently, a lot of labor consists of repetitive work — and we can use technology to liberate ourselves from this work and focus more of our energies on creative work.

One way to balance out this need for societal well-being within our current capitalistic system is to charge higher tax rates for companies that rely highly on capital rather than on labor. It's a way of re-calibrating contribution of capital and redirecting some of the gains into skilling up workforce that is replaced by AI. It sounds radical — but we also need to understand that human beings are more important than machines, and the way we are acting at the moment doesn't really show this view. We need to ask ourselves: Do we want to maximize shareholder value because capital is a scarce resource, or do we actually care about individual well-being? Keep in mind that different people have different views! In every type of business decision-making, we need to point out the risks of going too far. So before we implement a concept, let's discuss not only the benefits, but also the potential harm to societal well-being that may come along with it. This kind of debate should be built into our education systems because we need a holistic view for good decision-making. When the different actors in the product chain start to see the need for change, they can change their actions to craft a solution to these questions. Every individual is a decision maker. And as decision makers, we should still ask questions such as: Is this the best way for us to manage our company? If you think in a holistic way, you can always find ways to create win-win situations that will enhance societal well being and enable you to make good profits.

How would you inspire decision-makers in companies to pay for social well-being?

Let's say you are managing a thriving high tech company. You enjoy a great career because your team is also performing and supports your objectives well. Your company possesses a strong technology. The question I'd ask my students to reflect on is: What actually contributed to your company's and your success today? Your reasoning may start on the technical side — your technology is better than your competitors' products. If you look into the evolution of your technology, you can see that your technology is actually so great because there were many failures in the system; not necessarily only the ones in your own company, but those from competitors as well. The failures of others led to your learning! Thomas Edison said, "I haven't failed. I have just found 10,000 ways that did not work." This means, that you actually learned without having to incur the costs that these non-successful predecessors incurred in a process of trial and error that finally led to a stage of technology that is fruitful. Who should now pay for that experimentation cost?

When we broaden the scope of our analysis, we will easily see that our success is intertwined with the contributions of the ecosystem we are working in. How were you able to recruit such talented engineers to develop your product? Who were these people trained by? And this is not only speaking about educational institutions like schools and universities. You could also think about the families they grew up in — typically parents invest a lot of resources such as time and money into the education of their children. Some parents would even leave their home countries for their children to have a better future. That's a significant cost to the family. So your success is always only partially due to your own dedication, and very likely due to many fortunate circumstances provided by an ecosystem that many different actors paid for.

What else would you like to share?

I have two teenage children, and I believe that these years are very formative in their lives. I care about whether they are happy and whether they're moving in a direction that they will find fruitful for themselves. For me, this means that they need to understand the two deeply interconnected branches of a fruitful life: passion and meaning. If we only do what we enjoy but don't see a meaning in our work, we easily get bored. We will not enjoy fulfillment. If we only engage in meaningful work, and we aim only for creating a difference in other people's lives, we create a heavy burden for ourselves, and we will not be able to sustain our work for a long time. My son is really passionate about playing the piano. Listening to him reminds me of the limits of my teachings, of social sciences in general. I care very much about delivering impactful teaching to our students. I want to teach them how to have a holistic view about the consequences of their decisions. They eventually will be the entrepreneurs and managers, and in my view, they need to understand that every decision they make can have impact that extends beyond their particular field like finance or strategy because their decisions will also affect people in their organizations, their communities, and entire societies. My idea is that once students and future decision makers have understood this concept of interconnection, they will be more agreeable to paying back to society. Either by higher tax rates or other ways of intervention to help secure the health of the ecosystems that are needed for their companies and their children to prosper. It's a way to teach a reflection process, but not a solution. I think this is more sustainable.

And when I listen to my son playing classical pieces, it reminds me that there are always other means such as music that are so much more powerful to touch people's hearts than my research. This is a very humbling experience. It's okay, if I worked very hard and I still have not changed a lot. I encourage you to not have this expectation that you will ever find something that brings you happiness all the time. It's important for us to be able to cultivate a sense of happiness even when we feel out of place. There will always be moments even in your dream career, where you find you work repetitive and maybe boring, or extremely challenging and scary. Don't be scared of being stretched outside your comfort zone. It helps to now and then reflect on how much we have grown already. If you want to keep your happiness and your passion alive, do not use outcome as a measure for your work! There are so many people out there in our world who have passion, who have ideas, who are working very hard to change the world. And there are so many different forms of art and expression that can touch people's hearts and minds. Embrace the diversity of all the work of other people, to keep a healthy and happy life.

Beautiful brains change tomorrow...today
Brain-brush reflection exercise:

How did I feel when I read this?

What did I learn?

What will I integrate into my daily life?

What do you *really, really* want in life?

Luis Hanemann,
partner at e.ventures

What topic is currently on your mind?

I have spent some time researching about impact. What is positive impact? How do we create it? How do we measure it? And what is the role that companies and investors, or even the entire economy should play concerning impact?

When I started my research, I came across many articles that claimed "You can have it all." You can have the maximum positive environmental impact, social impact and financial impact. It sounded too good to be true. I think the definition of doing good or creating impact is still vague; everyone sees something different in it. At first, I found it a bit frustrating and maybe even a little bit intimidating, to see all these different ways to define impact. Depending on how people define impact, there are all these different ways of making positive impact work. Some people might say Tesla or Uber are positive impact companies: Uber eliminates the need for buying a car, and Tesla produces cars that do not pollute the environment. Other people would say they are the most destructive, capitalistic companies ever. In the end, I think you need to define for yourself what you see as positive impact, and what is not. So I dug a bit deeper, and I confirmed: "It's probably too good to be true." I came across so many players, I'd call them "greenwashing" companies, that just say they're doing good for PR purposes. In my experience, it's nearly impossible to do everything at once. You will have situations where you have to decide if you focus your energies more on the financial side or if you try to stay true to the origin of your mission.

Let's say you want to have impact on climate change, and therefore you decide to start a business that provides solar panels. After some time, you will face some situations where you have to decide whether you want to focus on spending more money on the financial side of operations or on the impact side. One example case would be: Do I improve my margins because then I'm financially stable and can invest more into research and development for improving the product, or do I want to keep the product as is and bring it to more people at a lower cost. Also, you need to decide how much salary you want to take out of the business. You need some income, to support your family and maybe your lifestyle, but every Euro you take out is a Euro you could have invested to generate more impact! Finally, you might be so successful, that other people want to buy your company, and you get an attractive offer. You'll need to decide if you take this offer and invest the extra money into another project that may create even more impact, or if you keep your business and follow your original values and mission.

What are a few examples of working impact models in business?

You have traditional models like Bosch, one of Germany's largest companies. No one owns Bosch, because Bosch owns itself by the way it's set up. It's owned by the Robert Bosch foundation, which channels the dividends it receives into charitable work. I don't think it's applicable for all industries in all business models, but I think it's definitely an interesting new way of running a business.

How you set up a company is a strategic decision. As a founder, you could even set up your company in a way where you can't even sell it anymore because it doesn't belong to you. There are also some more radical "purpose" business models on the market. You might have heard of Einhorn, the condom company from Berlin. They have decided to focus on delivering a concept called "fairstainability," which means aligning their corporate actions with the concept of fairness and sustainability along the value chain. The founders have contractually removed any managerial authority over their employees. They are thinking of changing their company into a model where even the founders don't own equity in the company itself. At least for now, all salaries are transparent to all employees.

Let's take another example, a company from Berlin called Coffee Circle. They started the company because they disliked the way coffee planters were treated in the industry. Not only were they treated badly in general, they were also exploited in the sense that they have all the work but someone else makes the money. The way they decided to create impact was to set up their business model in a way that would challenge the current system. They sell premium coffee. They get everything directly from the farmers, and so farmers can get better prices and reinvest this money into supporting their communities. I feel that companies like these can have a positive impact on coffee farmers. They reduce inequality inherent in the business system. And if you consider coffee farmers part of society, then you also have positive impact on society.

Challenging the current business model by cutting off the intermediaries can also lead to job losses. Isn't this a little bit of a simplistic view?

You're totally right about the unintended side effects. However, I think there are so many side effects, some of them we can't predict — so it's literally impossible to fully eradicate these risks. A great risk of thinking too much about all the possible unintended consequences is we never get started. The moment we are paralyzed by negative side effects, we leave the stage open for those who might be willing to take the risk and who might not think about ethics.

For me, impact means when I get into a situation and leave it again, the situation has changed for the better. Yes, let's think about possible side effects, and when we think, let's think thoroughly. What I do should have, in the long run, a positive impact on society. Let's have a sophisticated conversation about ethics, but then, let's act, because the potential cost of not acting is even higher. I'll leave the discussion about how to build global ethics to the experts, but what I can tell from my experience is that people do have a sense of what is right or wrong in life. In my view, most people know this, they just don't always act on it. There are so many social causes we need to solve. It could be anything from empowering women to reducing CO_2 emissions. I find the 17 Sustainable Development Goals, published by the UN, can provide a good starting point for drawing inspiration.

Why aren't there more of these business models in the market?

Because you don't profit so much from it, in a financial sense. I think, that even nowadays, our brains seem to seek financial success because it is wired to the notion of success. My online marketing agency, for example, is a more traditional one. It scaled nicely. In the beginning, we were four co-founders, and we grew to 70 people. We had growing revenues and good profits. Then we sold the company and got some good cash for it. Had I done so with one of these above mentioned purpose model, I don't think I could have sold the business and be where I am today, financially.

Another reason why I believe this purpose model is slow to adapt: it takes some efforts to design, implement, and scale businesses that challenge the way business has been done for the past few decades, if not centuries. You have to manage complex dynamics along with the ecosystem.

I do believe now though, that if basic needs are covered, people could be happy without earning much money. Having a purpose is at least equally important. And there are more and more people who are feeling the same.

Around two years ago, I met a professor of philosophy, Frithjof Bergmann, who has developed a concept called "New Work," and the central quote of his work is: "What do you really, really want?" In the eighties, General Motors announced they would need to lay off thousands of people in one of their major manufacturing closures in Detroit. Layoffs is something I believe we will see more of, in our near future. The professor and his research group received some funding to test a transition concept, where, instead of laying off half of the workers, all workers would only work for six months and would still get paid for the other six months while they didn't work. They created a self-development program, that included trainings, coaching, and so on, to help people make use of the free time to understand what they really wanted out of their lives. And it seemed that many of them found ways to build a new life from this.

I think to help large parts of societies transition into a digitized world, having more institutionalized models like the above mentioned that help you find what matters to you most is important. The career services provided by the German government are a starting point, but there is significant room to do so much more. For such a program to be effective, I think you need professional coaches that take people seriously. They need to be trained in helping people to figure out who they are and what they want in life.

What do you like most about your job as an investor?

Our role as an investor in internet startups is to find startups that have a chance to become successful and grow. So our role is to first find these startups, and then we help them achieve their mission. Investors differ a little bit across the board, but this concept is rather broad and I guess it's a good description of what the industry does.

What I definitely like about my job is having the opportunity to speak to so many people from different industries, different regions, different nations. So they have different views because they come from different cultural environments. In addition, they are mostly passionate, informed about their markets, and inspired by their mission, which, in turn, inspires me intellectually. I think we also foster a culture where we focus on enabling and empowering others, so we also create fairness in chances. The companies seem to enjoy working with us as their investors.

In our company, we decide in a consensus. This means, we sit around a table as an investment committee of people with different backgrounds. Everyone has a voice, and we make sure that we listen to each person's ideas. The most important driver for our decision is our evaluation of the team. Do we believe this founding team is capable of doing something big? Then, we also look at the market. Is the market big enough so that the company can grow? If these two criteria are met, we then go ahead with some more detailed analysis. We'd ask for sales and marketing data, and then run this data through our analysis tools to gain insights into what happens inside the company.

Growth in my industry means growth in the valuation of the company. As an example, when we invest into a company for ten million Euros, we will want to sell it maybe eight, nine, or ten years later for a couple of hundred million or even a billion Euro. Our job, at least in this current system that we are playing, is to deliver financial return. In order for a startup to deliver financial return, the market needs to be big enough and the team strong enough to support exponential growth. We need this growth because, in the startup world, not all startups succeed. Let's say, we invest in twenty companies, ten might go bankrupt, and five may just be financially okay. Out of the remaining five, we need at least one to three financial outliers just to make sure our portfolio is healthy.

When it comes to the founding team, our job is to evaluate not only if the founding team has the capability to think big. We also evaluate, if the team has the capability to learn fast and is therefore able to adapt to the ever-changing dynamics of the environment. Nothing ever works from A to B in a direct way, in particular in fast paced environments like the internet industry. Finally, we think they have to be dedicated to coping with failures along the way. We are looking for this mindset that says: "Okay, we're eating shit at the moment, but we're going to get out!" For us, we have a "no asshole" policy. When we think the market is big, the founding team is capable, but we also think they are assholes, then we just won't invest. And this is where it becomes more of an art than data.

How do you evaluate founders' mindsets?

It's not that structured of a process. But there are some clues, like, how aware team members are of their skills and failings. You may be a person who is a great product person, but you may be lacking some sales experience. What this could lead to is you have a perfectly designed product, but you struggle to bring it to people. So what we do is check if the team will be open to bringing in someone that provides this missing expertise, or would any of them be willing to learn this skill?

Another clue is how people react to new ideas or questions from outside of the team. I'd associate openness with willingness to listen first and understand where the other person is coming from. I can share two different scenarios, so you can maybe understand more clearly what I mean.

In a feedback session, company one might say: "Hey, that's valuable input. We'd see problems implementing your suggestions for x, y, z. What are your thoughts on this — how can we still make it work?" So in this way, we can have a conversation about how to change. On the other spectrum, company two might say something like: "Sorry, this won't work out. This is how we do it, and this the only way we're going to do it." With such a mindset, it will be difficult to run a growing organization. People who are not open to listening are also difficult to coach. And coaching is a big lever to learning.

I think founders nowadays are more collaborative — this means they are more open to sharing an honest view about their current status. And they would also more openly ask for help in areas where they feel they lack expertise. More importantly, they know better in which way we can help them. For us, it helps understand what they can deliver and what they won't deliver. In a sense, it reduces information inefficiencies. In earlier times, founders would try to hide their blind spots and pretend to be in full control of everything. There was this common belief it was a founder's job to know it all.

Why is it important to listen to other people?

I think we need to listen to other people because this is one important way to learn. We understand our world through other people. We are by design dependent on others — we are not pure individuals. The way we see things is influenced by other people. If my friends say, "You're successful," then I might see myself as successful. What determines my value system today is also in part influenced by the value system that my parents taught me.

In a traditional sense, we'd view ourselves in relation to our family, then maybe the community we live in, and we can expand to the country we live in. If you look at it from a humanistic view, there are no limits — you could keep on expanding. Sometimes I feel responsible for everything and everyone. It's a pleasure, and sometimes it's also a big burden because I know that there is always somewhere some suffering. So you need to find your own balance, how much of it you want to care about.

Without listening or talking to other people, we can't be human. So listening is also a way to take responsibility for others. When we listen, we can understand what others need, and we can help them if needed. That's my take on responsibility. First, you have a responsibility to yourself. That's priority number one because if you know what makes you act the way you act, can you understand human systems. A human system is you in connection to other people. Understanding yourself will help you understand others, which makes communication easier.

In entrepreneurship, listening is important, for instance, when you want to test a new idea. When there is something that catches my attention, I dig deeper. What I do is try to learn as much about it as possible by reading and reaching out to people who may have more knowledge in this field. When I meet these people, I ask them all the stupid questions I have, and then, step by step, when I feel I have understood the concept, the idea, or their belief system, I also see how it relates to me and my belief system. Let's say you want to start a coaching company. If I were you, I'd go around reaching out to people and communicating in a way as if I already had this coaching company. I'd say: "Hey, I have this service — would you be interested in trying it?" When you know how to listen well to your potential customers and experts in the field, you can tweak your product fast until you have something that feels ready to launch.

What are the limits of the current decision-making model or the current ecosystem?

I see thousands of limits. Focusing on material growth is definitely one of the drivers of our own limitations. In some way it inhibits creative thinking. Let's say someone has a great idea and I also believe in this person, still, at some point along the way, we will have to face how this idea will make money. Many of us will wonder, "How are you going to finance your life?" One of the ways to remove the income pressure from someone's life is through basic universal income; it's another tweak to the Frithjof Model I mentioned above. I find it appealing because it would enable people to have enough money in their life to go and explore where their heart, their passion leads.

In general, people are not made for thinking globally. We're not made for thinking in groups of millions of people. I don't think our brains are capable of creating solutions that are universally applicable. We are limited by design. On a positive node — just reflecting on our cognitive limitations, and seeing the progress we as humanity have made so far, it's not that bad, is it?

What I've seen working well to create acceptable solutions is to bring people together, let them talk, think through stuff together, debate. When things don't work, more often than not they come from a place of prejudice. It's not only in the work environment where this can have negative impact on outcome — you can also see it in politics. The way good progress happens, in my view, is to by bringing in a diverse amount of people and working together. Their different thoughts, their different perspectives will have a good impact on the outcome. When we have an open and curious learning mindset and when we have respect for others, even when they have completely different views, we all gain. If you only engage with people from similar age ranges, backgrounds, professions, then you are not going to have an enriching life.

So that's why in our company, we cultivate the view that everyone has the right to be treated equally. This means I try to be fair, transparent, and open in my interaction with others; and it does not mean that we will tolerate harmful behavior to others!

Anything else you want to share with us?

In general, I don't think we would be happy people if we didn't have anything to do. We need to have goals and progress to be happy. Some need more, some need less, but I don't think it must be paid work. I think people need a purpose to be happy in life. They need to sense that what they do is meaningful — and this may be completely different to you than it is to me. And that is okay too!

So one of the things I would recommend to everyone is to ask yourself: what's really, really important for you? What do you really, really want in your life or in your career? And if you ask that question not only once, but at different stages in your life, you will come to different answers too. I'm still in the process, which means I don't know 100 percent myself what it is I really, really want. What I know at this stage is that I want to focus more of my energy on solving problems that cater to creating a positive impact on society. Throughout my career, that was not always the case; and I keep on learning a lot about myself.

One caveat: While I love ambitious people, I also think that reflecting thoroughly about what we can realistically achieve in this world can help us find grounding. I try to not take myself too seriously when I get stressed about things. I think, "I'm one of seven billion people on this planet, and I'm here, and I'll probably stay here for a couple of more decades. Whatever I do, it's not going to change the world massively." It sounds a bit funny, but it relaxes me. Understanding, that there have been so many people before me on this planet, and there will be so many people after me, brings back a bit of humbleness into my everyday life. Sometimes it's not a bad idea to align heart and mind. Then you act upon it.

Beautiful brains change tomorrow...today
Brain-brush reflection exercise:

How did I feel when I read this?

What did I learn?

What will I integrate into my daily life?

Dear beloved reader, thank you for being part of our journey towards living a peaceful life.

I invite you to breathe, smile, and thank yourself for being such a wonderful human being. Your presence is a gift to the earth.

You are, therefore I am, the way I am. I love you.

Further reading mentioned in the interviews:

Achor, Shawn. *Big Potential*.
mentioned in the chapter by Dr. Kerstin Humberg

Achor, Shawn. *The Happiness Advantage*.
mentioned in the chapter by Dr. Kerstin Humberg

Blanton, Brad. *Radical Honesty*.
mentioned in the chapter by Urs Merkel

Dalio, Ray. *Principles*.
mentioned in the chapter by Dr. Kerstin Humberg

Frankl, Victor. ***Man's Search for Meaning***.
mentioned in multiple chapters

Hardy, Darren. *The Compound Effect.*
mentioned in the chapter by Dr. Tu-Lam Pham

Kahneman, Daniel. *Thinking Fast and Slow*.
mentioned in the chapter by Nikolas Schriefer

Pauli, Gunter. *Blue Economy*.
mentioned in the chapter by Luca Urbano

Pink, Daniel. *Drive*.
mentioned in the chapter by Dr. Tu-Lam Pham

Painted by
Alla Golovanova

About Yip

Thy-Diep (Yip) is committed to helping individuals and organizations improve decision-making and well-being in a systemic way (body, mind, soul). Aiming to gain integral understanding of human systems, she has throughout her life honed her skills working in different roles for a diverse portfolio of corporations, startups and not-for-profit institutions.

She is a trainer and business (neuro-) coach, designing interactions built on mindfulness practice, body work and neurosciences. Previously, she worked as a management consultant for McKinsey&Co, where she served C-Level executives from insurance, banking, telco and public sector.

She is Chief Well-Being Officer at brainboost, a neurotechnology company that commits itself to advancing the UN "Agenda 2030" Sustainable Development Goals #3: good health and well-being, #4: quality education and #17: global partnerships.

Reach out to Yip if you want to understand how to bring mindful decision-making processes into your organization.

www.beautifulbrains.club
contact@beautifulbrains.club

Connect with Thy-Diep (Yip) at
linkedin.com/in/thydiepta

Learn more about Amie at
amiemccracken.com

47943400R00153

Printed in Poland
by Amazon Fulfillment
Poland Sp. z o.o., Wrocław